A Year of Losing the Dating Game

by Samantha Bye

A big thanks to the friends who have laughed at my dating stories over the years and told me this book is a good idea.

Special thanks also go to the men who unknowingly took part. Without you, I'd be less dead inside but this book wouldn't exist so every cloud.

This is a table of contents

The Opening Chapter 6

A Useful Index 7

A Bit About Me 9

A Bit About My Sexual History 12

A Bit About The Challenge 14

The End of the Year of Celibacy 16

WANTED: One Man to Mount Me Regularly 24

The Night I Realised I'm a Great Player 29

The Inevitable Pie and the Aftermath 34

Getting Over One by Getting Under Another 39

Groundwork January 46

Getting Back in the Game 49

Another Successful Weekend of Being a Player ... 58

The One Who Could Have Ended the Book 71

When the Shit Hit the Fan 95

An Open Letter to Mr Disappointment 122

The Return and Speedy Exit of Mr Disappointment
.... 129

The Cancelled Dates 137

The Birth of 15 Matches, 1 Question and the Sudden Influx of Toyboys 142

The Sexual Reawakening and the End of Polite-Mode 157

The Mid-Year Review 163

The Second Half Setup 167

The Worst Date in the History of All Dating Ever 175

The Man League 181

Desperate Times Call For Desperate Measures . 189

Dropping Like Flies 192

The End of a Slow Summer 198

Fucked Over by Karma 204

Fucked Over by Karma (Part 2) 208

The End of the Dry Spell 215

The Night of Realisations 224

The Big Dicked Perv 228

The Week of Shit Men 231

Our First Organic Man 237

Another One Plays the Long Game 242

The Hazy Date with Mr RE Man 249

The Aftermath and a Series of Unanswered Questions 256

A Touch of Déjà vu 261

If in Doubt, Get 'em Out for the Delusional Men .. 264

The Date That Made Me Question My Life 269
Changing My Dating Technique 278
The Final Stretch 281
New Year, New Me 287

The Opening Chapter

It was a cold December evening. My mind was wandering and restless, and I needed a new hobby to occupy some time. I started thinking about what I'm good at and what I enjoy. Sex is good. I like writing. Let's go on a year-long dating mission and write about it. Simple. I may as well get laid whilst being productive.

My encounters with men up until this point in my life have either been amusing or tragic stories rather than something to make other women feel jealous, as my bad luck mixed with my fear of settling has never conjured up anything of substance. It's because of this that I thought, rather than having this trickling flow of stories to tell to my friends, why not crank it up a gear and tell the whole world about it? I'm not desperate for a relationship and I definitely don't feel like I've experienced enough men to feel satisfied about sticking to just one, so maybe at the end of this I'll be ready to honour my mother's wishes and settle down like a respectable young lady. Then again, maybe not, but it'll be great fucking fun finding out.

A Useful Index

In this book, there are a lot of websites, apps and social media platforms mentioned. Just in case you're not familiar with them, I've created this.

Facebook – Don't be ridiculous, everyone knows Facebook.

Instagram – A social media just for pictures. Mainly selfies, great dogs, inspirational quotes, and funny shit (but that could just be me). You can add filters to the pictures to make you look a lot more attractive than you actually are.

Match.com – A dating website that you have to pay for. Complete waste of money, more weirdos and bad people on this one than any other.

Plenty of Fish (POF) – A free online dating site. Full of settlers, the dregs of society, and pictures of men's penises.

Snapchat – An app perfect for sending ugly selfies and nudes. Images disappear after a few seconds unless they're screenshotted.

Tinder – A free dating app. Requires no input of personal information, instead you just swipe left for no if they're ugly and right for yes if they're shaggable. If you both find each other attractive enough to mutually swipe right you get a 'match'. Only matches can exchange words. Then numbers. Then nude pictures.

WhatsApp – A messaging app that feeds everyone's inner stalker. There is a time stamp to see when people were last online, and a blue tick to show when they read it so you know exactly when you're being ignored.

A Bit About Me

It's only fair that I tell you a bit about myself now, so you can get to know me before we delve into this. First for the basics:

I'm 24 years old and have never had a serious relationship.

I probably could have once or twice but I get bored of people quickly and I'm too independent to go out with someone for the sake of having a relationship. Not that it's all been my choice of course, I can fully confess to having a few pies thrown in my face over the years.

I can admit to being 7 out of 10 on a good day.

This book isn't me saying 'I'm so fit, look at all these men I can mug off' as I won't even pretend that's the case. I'm slightly (about four stone) overweight, am a borderline midget at 5'2, and don't have the patience to spend half my life on my appearance.

Saying that, I do have quite a nice face. Especially when I take a picture and Instagram the shit out of it.

I think like a man.

Which makes this challenge seem like a piece of piss. I don't get attached easily, I'm crude in the way I describe things, and my laidback attitude along with my sense of humour lures in the right kind of men required for this challenge. This skill allows me to see straight through bullshit as well (along with very impressive social media stalking abilities), so watching men make excuses and tell lies is quite amusing when I already know the truth.

Also, I read Cosmo like, all the time so I know exactly what to do to make men love me (in theory, yet to apply this in practice.)

Even if I did want a relationship, it would take a special man to be able to handle me.

I do have a strong personality and I don't want to be tamed. I like being me. I don't want to have to tone it down or pretend to be the certain type of woman that everyone wants for the sake of pleasing a man. For that reason, there aren't many men who could handle me and I'm ok with that.

I also don't want to be with someone who'll just put up with the whole me without joining my level. I'd get bored of someone who doesn't really get it and I would probably (unintentionally) walk all over them.

A Bit About My Sexual History

I didn't lose my virginity until I was 20.

I spent all of my teenage years waiting for 'The One'. During university I gradually learnt that love is a myth and human beings are just fucking awful to each other, but I still held my faith…

… And then I went to Magaluf and smashed three men in five days because I was drunk, horny, and feared I'd be a virgin forever. No regrets.

I've never slept with the same man on more than one occasion.

Yep, I am the Queen of One Night Stands. No, I do not think sex equals love and haven't shagged everyone hoping they'll be my boyfriend. There have been people I've liked where I've held off thinking that's what normal people who want relationships do and then it's never worked out. Not because I've been a frigid little bitch for ages, but because I've spotted they're massive arseholes before I've let them in my knickers.

The point about me never having a serious relationship comes into play again here. Pies have been thrown both ways, so some people haven't wanted to have another go on me and vice versa.

Until recently, I'd never even seen someone I'd had sex with again. The one who broke this streak reminded me why.

A Bit About The Challenge

The end of 2013 confirmed that relationships really aren't for me.

I will outline fully what happened during the last few months of last year in the following chapters, but here's the basic outline of what happens to me. The men I do get that rare feeling of attachment for let me down and decide they don't want me. No I'm not crying the victim, it's just what happens. Maybe I do get attached to the wrong people but I'm weird and awkward so naturally I love men that are the same. Unfortunately, they too are mentally unstable and it never works. All the other men make great stories.

Only a certain calibre of man will be accepted.

I've made a rule that I'm not willing to go lower than 6/10. Also they need to be able to hold a conversation, otherwise they don't get to see my amazing personality and it's more difficult to reel them in or I lose interest in flogging them for the sake of a poor to average chapter. Characters are what we're looking for, not mere notches on the bed post.

My head is in business-only mode.

I'm not in it for the love; I'm in it for the book. I shall be shutting down all emotions and playing the Ice Queen as best I can.

That being said, if someone with a rugby player body and the sex appeal of Ryan Gosling asks me to marry them this idea is Romeo done and will forever lurk in the dark depths of my hard drive. I'm not a complete moron.

There's a strong chance my stomach will let me down on numerous occasions.

Sometimes I reach a point with people where the thought of them being inside me (be it for round one, round two, or beyond) physically turns my stomach. I can't continue with a person once this happens. I don't know why it happens but I like to think it's my built-in moral compass telling me I've gone too far and to abort mission. Once that point is reached it'll be onto the next one.

Now with all that said, let's get into the arse-end of 2013 shall we? Read on…

The End of the Year of Celibacy

When I haven't had sex for a while I kind of forget about it. Like a distant memory, it becomes something I once had and something I can do without. Until I stumble upon it again. And this was definitely a stumble thanks to approximately seven litres of vodka and the danger juice that is Sambuca. This encounter is the motivation for this book, the reason why I have been putting it about a bit, and where my desire to be a player for the next 12 months has come from. My sexual need has been awoken and the flame of passion has turned into an absolute beast of a fire that no amount of cock can put out.

Whilst on holiday in September, I celebrated my one year anniversary of celibacy. I didn't make a conscious decision to go without sex, I just hadn't looked for it and no one came up to me on the street to offer it so me and my vagina went without.

A few weeks after returning home, me and a friend decided to go out on a school night to see a

DJ (I'm not at school but work still permitted me to be up at 6.30am the following day. This was never going to end well). When we got there, we remembered it was Freshers Week and hammered louty students were everywhere. Rather than putting my sensible head on and calling it a night, I panic drank. Suddenly I was one of them. I fitted in, and I was having a wonderful time.

And then I saw him. Mr Cheater. We work together and he most certainly has a girlfriend. Wobbling over to say hello, nothing seemed untoward. Even when his friends announced they were going home and he claimed he'd be staying with me, I saw nothing of it but a friendly exchange. It was around this time that shots were mentioned. I told him Sambuca makes me weird so what proceeded to happen wasn't really my fault. I'd given the warning. My actions were to be taken out of my control. We danced, drank more, and laughed. He's very attractive and my drunken one-track mind forgot about his girlfriend. Apparently so did his.

He started it. As we sat and chatted, he gave me possibly the most unique compliment I've ever received. "You're really hot in a weird way." Pardon? Drunk Me only heard the first bit. The next day, Sober Me heard it all. What does that even mean? Am I a guilty crush like fucking Vanessa Feltz or something? At least everyone can tell I've got a bit of character from the outset of meeting me I suppose no matter how hard I try to cage it.

Once that was said we both knew which way it was going. Apparently I dragged him home with me (not that he protested in any way shape or form), and just in case I had any doubt about what was to happen one flashback allows me to recall the way he looked at me as he sat on my bed and I changed into my pyjamas. Yep, I put my pyjamas on. Because nothing says 'stick it in me' quite like comfortable nightwear. His drunken eyes were already taking them off me. Who's the weird one now, buddy?

As soon as I got into bed he was on top of me. I only have a few fleeting flashbacks of the incident itself but from what I do remember it was quite possibly the best sex I have ever had. Although saying that, being better than previous lovers isn't actually that hard as I am, after all, The Queen of One Night Stands and have quite often had to ask men to "hurry up and finish, and get off me". It was intense, he was a nice size (it's not satisfying unless I'm sore the next day), and that's about as much as I recall. Apart from one move. One move which caused people to snort in shock and disgust when I told them. One move which took an awful lot of careful explaining to ensure the exact manoeuvre and execution was understood. I'll tell you what I told them. Imagine The Human Centipede but without the tears and with two willing candidates.

It's unfortunate that I remember this part of the act in so much detail. Especially as I love to share and no one wants to hear about it. He flipped me over onto my front, shuffled down, and put his whole face between my legs. Brilliant, now I have to face someone at work every day that's had not only their penis, but also their whole head inside my cervix. And this, my dear readers, is the first person I'd ever slept with and seen again. I'm not sure what part of this is worse, the thought of his nose being almost completely inside my anus or the fact that I wasn't expecting to be naked that evening so hadn't shaved a single hair off my body for at least three weeks. I was a yeti on all fours; he was half the size of me lapping it up, quite literally, like a scrawny boy who hadn't eaten in a week.

When I woke up at 6.30am the next day (still remembered to set my alarm, I deserve a fucking pay rise), the standard hangover confusion of "where am I and who the bloody hell is next to me?" wasn't present. I later discovered that this was because I was still hammered and stayed that way until at least 10am - an hour and a half after I'd arrived at my desk (maybe I don't deserve that pay rise after all). I got ready for work and woke up Mr Cheater before unsuccessfully searching for his lost wallet and ushering him out of the door to prevent my poor mother from spotting him.

We took the bus together, my treat as his wallet was nowhere to be found, and practised the hangover deep breathing while he got into the foetal position across two chairs in front of me and puked all over them. There was absolutely nothing good about this morning.

I was sussed out almost instantly when I got into work. I stank of alcohol and sex, and my neck was completely covered in love bites. What kind of self-respecting 24 year old woman lets a man exercise his inner vampire all over her neck?! They're not acceptable unless you're 16 or under, and even then it's still not alright. Keeping my mouth shut about who the lucky man had been was tough, but not as tough as trying not to be sick. I lasted until 1pm on the latter, and promptly left shortly after. Sitting with my face on my desk on top of the state I came into work in, is apparently not regarded as professional behaviour.

As well as all this, there was still one matter that needed to be tended to. Contraception: or the lack of it. Getting carried away is one thing, getting pregnant is another, so rather than being able to go home and die in bed I had to swallow my pride and go to collect the morning after pill. I don't embarrass easily, but crawling through the doors of the pharmacy not only smelling of booze and sex but sick now too, with love bites on my neck and my sleep-deprived, hungover eyes bulging out my head wasn't one of my finest moments. It didn't help that the poor sod who served me was undoubtedly still a virgin, so watching him squirm and turn an impressive shade of pink whilst asking "when did the incident occur?", as if it wasn't obviously the night before enough, added to what could only be described as a solid 2 out of 10 day.

It didn't end there. When I finally did get into bed I stumbled upon Mr Cheater's lost wallet. Typical. Our drunken states in the morning forced us to overlook what was right in front of our eyes. I was hoping to get my James Bond on around the office to avoid him for the rest of my life but a face-to-face encounter was now inevitable. My whole weekend was spent full of dread, shame, walking like a cowboy, and trying to disguise all of this in front of my immediate family. How was he going to explain this to his girlfriend? What if he tells her? She's scary and will definitely rip my face off. I'm such a bad person.

Despite all my panicking, the wallet exchange wasn't as horrendous as I was expecting. Another winning point was that even though he came to my desk to collect it, no one on the team suspected a thing. I think I've got away with this.

All of our brief exchanges after this were awkward but manageable. No substantial conversations took place, we were able to say 'hello' without anyone around us suspecting we'd done the sex, and our paths rarely crossed.

Until the work Christmas party. He was completely intoxicated from arrival and I noticed his eyes following me all over the room. I knew it was wrong, but the danger made me want round two even more. I worked on it, and the more I worked on it I realised just how drunk he was. If I were to take him home it would probably be considered illegal. Because of this, I found someone else to take me home instead (but more on that later).

As I was waiting for my lift to arrive, I noticed Mr Cheater outside all over another girl. Now ladies I'm sorry for the lack of sisterly girl power here, but this new victim was what I can only describe as an absolute beast. Is he some kind of chubby chaser? Why do men with super-hot girlfriends do this? Was I a pig that needed to be conquered? One thing I know for sure is that this guy is case closed.

WANTED: One Man to Mount Me Regularly

You know the saying 'once you pop, you just can't stop'? Well after the antics with Mr Cheater, I felt the meaning of this saying in full force. Unfortunately, I had no available and willing men lined up to cure the constant throb on I was carrying around, almost leading me to hump inanimate objects in public and drool over anything I spotted that was phallic-shaped.

    I had tried internet dating before and it had been completely fruitless, but with no other options I put on my optimistic head and wrote a witty, interesting profile, and uploaded all of my best (potentially slightly misleading) pictures to Plenty of Fish. During this stint, there were two men worthy of a mention. I'm sure there were other ones I spoke to or some notable weirdos that were good to laugh at for a few seconds, but the latter comes in thick and fast and they all merge into one soul-destroying ball that my mind automatically shoves into my subconscious to prevent me from the depression of hideously ugly men thinking they've got a chance.

First up was Mr No Charisma. This lack of charisma was evident from the outset but unfortunately I was thinking with my vagina the whole time which prevented me from noticing it. The first night we started talking, numbers were exchanged and we spent two hours on the phone talking. Aw nice, you must think. He was on his Xbox the whole time. Always nice when a man trying to woo you gives you half of his attention isn't it?

Regardless of this we continued to talk for a week or so and a lunch date was arranged. On the morning, I got up early, made myself look extra-hot, and psyched myself up as I hadn't had a proper date in seven years due to my streak of 'get drunk and have sex' encounters. After all this, I didn't hear from him. Lunch hours are precious when you work in an office so when 12pm struck, I went to lunch without him. He then called me when I had 15 minutes left, and rather than be gutted to have missed me or even slightly apologetic like he fucking should have been, his words were "can you just meet me in town quick and give me a fag?" Charming.

I had told him numerous times that I had an operation approaching which was going to leave me out of action for three weeks. This was something he either didn't care much about or just couldn't get his head round. However, a lunch date was rescheduled for two days before surgery was due. The same pattern as the previous date day morning followed and I text him with details on where and when to meet me. His van broke down and he couldn't get to work. Great. He told me he'd let me know whether he managed to get it moving but an hour before we were due to meet I still hadn't heard from him. I text him asking what he was doing and he replied "Van isn't working. I'm at home."

Sounds like a right bellend doesn't he? It gets worse. The day of my operation came round and I heard nothing from him. Now, I'm not a needy person but I'm a big fan of decency and I believe the decent thing to do would have been to text me wishing me well. Nope, instead I heard from him three days later with a text that read "You better yet?" When I reminded him for the 796th time that I was not going to be available for three weeks, he offered "something to make me smile". "No I don't want a picture of your cock thanks" I said. Apparently men don't like a woman they've never met politely declining a picture of their genitals. "Oh I'm sick of girls like you. Bore me later." Girls like me who don't want a picture of your cock? So, all girls ever in the world then? Good luck getting anyone to agree to be your girlfriend mate.

Mr No Charisma fizzled out shortly after and was replaced by Mr Out of Proportion.

When Mr Out of Proportion first messaged me I was sceptical. His pictures were slightly blurry, I couldn't work out if he was a bit weird, but I gave him my number a few messages deep anyway. He caught me in a generous mood, clearly. It didn't take long for me to be glad of this generous mood. Within days we were up texting until the early hours and were talking on the phone like we'd known each other for years. He was the first man in a long time that I genuinely couldn't find a negative for, which although sounds silly as we hardly knew each other, is very rare for a natural human-hater such as myself.

As we'd started talking just after my operation, it was difficult to arrange a proper date but after a week I agreed to meet him at a quiet bar down the road from my house as I was keen to meet him and he seemed keen to meet me too. However, the day before I didn't hear a single thing from him. Very unusual considering we were texting from waking to sleeping every day. The next day I text asking if we were still on for the drink and he gave me a shit excuse then ignored me for a week. I convinced myself that he'd Facebook stalked me, decided he thought I was fat, and didn't fancy it anymore. Not all that far-fetched a theory when he reinstated his account the night before, asked what my full name was, then asked "What clothes size are you by the way? Not that it matters." Whether or not this was the real reason we'll never know but I was genuinely quite gutted.

    A week later and I woke up to a text from him. In essence, he wasn't ready for a relationship and wanted something 'fun and casual'. I definitely never said anything about wanting a serious relationship, but what does fun and casual mean? Is that just sex or…? I was so confused I even Googled it, but even Google couldn't give me the answer. I sent a long message back asking what he meant, feeling ready to discuss it, and wished him a happy birthday. It took him two hours to write "Ok. Thanks!" ARE YOU KIDDING ME? And that was the end of him. Kind of.

The Night I Realised I'm a Great Player

Once I'd recovered from my operation, a friend's birthday night out was on the cards. Obviously this meant I was going to be trawling the dance floor for cock, and that I did.

By the time we got out out (via the casino first) I was already quite drunk and the gin confidence was out in full force but no one was biting. Very disappointing considering I looked quite fit that night. I strutted around, giving the eyes to any faces I could tolerate being on top of me, but it just wasn't happening. With no other option there was only one thing for it. Drunk dialling.

I held off until about 1am before the standard "Where are you?" texts went shooting off to both Mr No Charisma and Mr Out of Proportion. Both bit the bait and my drunken persuasion for them to pick me up and take me home was out in full force. Don't you just love how alcohol allows us all to play it cool in the finest form? If I'm honest, I didn't even need to beg. The question was posed, quite straightforwardly, to both of them and I was then made aware of just how much men really do think with their dicks. If a drunken girl offers it no matter how sober they are they will throw morals out the window and will already have themselves balls deep inside you in their mind.

    Mr Out of Proportion was on a night out about an hour away but was driving and said he wouldn't be able to pick me up until about 4am, like I'm going to sit in the street for three hours and wait. He eventually left his night out early and asked for my location but by this time I'd already managed to get Mr No Charisma out of bed to pick me up. "Too late, my back-up has arrived" I text him. To say he was unimpressed is an understatement. The club wouldn't let him back in and he was soberly stranded in the middle of the street with the promise of fanny drifting away from his grasp. In essence he then told me to fuck off which I suppose is quite fair.

    Mr No Charisma was exactly as I'd expected him to be: an absolute bellend. But at least I didn't have to pay for a taxi, every cloud. When he pulled up to my house he decided he wasn't coming in because my mum and brother were asleep inside but rather than this being a gentlemanly gesture, he stuck his tongue in my mouth then told me to get in the back of his van. No amount of gin could have made me do that as even I could never be horny enough to be made to feel like a kidnap victim. So I gave him a firm no which caused him to throw a strop and plead "are you at least going to suck me off?" I got out the van without answering and he huffed off back to bed.

What happened next was perfect timing at its best. Fifteen minutes had passed since Mr Out of Proportion told me to fuck off. I'd just stepped out of Mr No Charisma's van, and the former then text me again saying "Can I please just come and see you?" Actually sir, yes you can. You can come inside me as well, I thought, but I managed to act as if that wasn't on the cards as men fucking love a challenge and I didn't want to jinx the inevitable pounding that would occur should he take the hour trip to my place.

I gave him my address and he insisted on calling me during the drive to ensure I didn't fall asleep while he was on his way. As we chatted he told me he'd missed talking to me. I'd missed talking to him too so the hour long conversation was almost like foreplay. As he was approaching I stood outside to greet him, and when he got out of his car I remembered an article I'd read which said that the main thing men lie about on their online dating profiles is their height. Mr Out of Proportion had told me he's 5'6" but there's no way he was taller than the 5'2" me. Good job I'd taken my heels off or I'd have felt like I was sneaking in a child.

Height doesn't matter when you're both horizontal though does it? We chatted in bed for about 47 seconds before genitalia was being pulled out all over the place, and this is where you learn the meaning of this one's name. Although small in height, this dude had the biggest fucking penis I've ever seen both in length and girth. In fact, I think my vagina may have clenched in fear when I first fondled the goods.

I think he understood that a good amount of warming up was needed on my part before he stuck his weapon in me, as going in slightly dry would have definitely caused a long term injury. So as he got to work on that I laid back and said a prayer for my cervix. Round one went reasonably well, despite him saying "I love being inside you" as he entered. I am not a fan of men attempting to dirty talk so I did do a slight cringe at that point. The sex hurt a bit but I was still able to gain some form of pleasure from it as his back was in shreds afterwards. Round two, however, was far too ambitious. It felt like I was being mutilated by a butternut squash.

One thing that must be said about Mr Out of Proportion is that his control was quite incredible. When the moment came for me to call time, I told him to finish and he was done. Just like that. Voice controlled penis, very impressive.

He left at 5.45am as he had work at 6.30am. He then sat through a ten hour shift in last night's clothes stinking of sex. Before he left we went back to his previous text mentioning 'fun and casual' and agreed that's what we'll do. I liked this idea; having a fuck buddy seems so grown up and it meant I'd finally be sleeping with someone on more than one occasion! Maybe I'm not shit at sex and ugly in person after all.

When I got up the next morning I acted normal with the family and soon realised my late night caller had gone completely undetected. I was a sex ninja, and I was so proud of myself. My vagina however, was not proud and bled for three days afterwards. That damn massive penis.

The Inevitable Pie and the Aftermath

I never heard from Mr No Charisma again after that night, thank god. But me and Mr Out of Proportion continued to text through the week. Unsurprisingly though, the tone of the conversation had changed and it was all about sex. There wasn't even "how are you?" just "sit on my face" and other such pleasantries. But I knew where I stood and I rolled with it, making plans for another drunken booty call the next weekend.

The plans for round two were set. I even went and bought some lube and a box of tissues to put next to my bed in preparation. "Look at me, being one of them people getting regular sex!" I thought. On the day, we were texting up until the early evening and gave it the old "see you later!" It was arranged for him to meet me in town, but after not hearing from him for hours I finally got the text. "Ah Sam, I don't think I can come but I don't want to be a let down :(I'm sorry x".

The best way to not be a let down is to explain yourself and your stupid fucking cryptic message. The best way to not be a let down would be to answer your damn phone when the person you're letting down tries to call you straight after you've sent the message. Shit, the best way to not be a let down is to NOT BE A FUCKING LET DOWN. To this day, I still have no idea of his reasoning. I never heard from him again.

Unfortunately, when I'm drunk and angry I go straight into self-destructive mode. I was going to have sex with the first person I could get my hands on, and within an hour I'd already found and secured my victim. I call him a victim, but I was probably making myself a victim at his hands.

I can't remember his name but I started talking to him and there was absolutely nothing special about him. He was an arrogant arsehole not even worth a special book name. He was visiting from out of town and had a room in a local Travelodge so I went back with him.

We got down to business fairly quickly and I found out he had no condoms. I still wasn't on the pill at this point either. Ladies let me tell you, when a stranger is aware of your complete lack of contraception and promises not to come inside you, he will still fucking come inside you. Twice. Thanks for that mate. He also won't offer to pay for the morning after pill, and will ask you to leave before his friends come back.

Between the sex and the departure, I may have smoked a fair bit of weed with him out of the hotel window. I sound more and more like a skanky whore with every sentence don't I? When I left, I went to the hotel reception and asked them to call me a taxi. As the reality of what I'd just done hit me I sat down with my eyes bulging out my head trying not to cry as I'd never felt more like a piece of meat. Worst night ever. The reception man took pity on me and gave me a bottle of water though so that was quite nice.

I spent all of the next day hating myself and calling all of my friends to make me feel better. However, you can't keep this dog down for long so the Monday morning I got up early before work, got the morning after pill, treated myself to a coffee and pastry, and took a minute to enjoy it in the park before the working week started. I was in a great mood now because food makes me happy and I was almost definitely not going to have a bastard child.

There was one thing I did think about occasionally through the week though which of course was Mr Out of Proportion. There is nothing worse than being pied off twice by the same man, with no explanation either time. What I do love to do though is to get a bit of revenge. I'm not really the kind of girl to walk away after being mugged off so doing something that I find hilarious is like a coping mechanism. In my opinion, being the bigger person and walking away doesn't make you the bigger person. It makes you the person who got shat on and let someone get away with it.

A few days into the week I went to a friend's house for dinner. She was on Plenty of Fish and being the good friend I am, I went onto her account and started sending horrendous messages to people. "I want to do a shit on your chest", "When are we fucking then?" and other obscenities were sent to poor unsuspecting men, and although horrified at first, my friend found it funny after a bottle of wine and allowed me to continue in exchange for full rights to my Tinder account for the evening.

She then had a great idea to get these men to send us pictures of their cocks. Although it wouldn't be our numbers we'd give them, oh no. We gave them the number of Mr Out of Proportion. The number was given to approximately 20 men, and one weirdo even called and left a voicemail of him wanking. Men are such filthy bastards. A few messages with a random girl online and they're ready and willing to send a picture of their cock in the hope of maybe getting a picture of tits back.

    Mr Out of Proportion hadn't been on WhatsApp for a few hours so must have looked at his phone a few hours later and seen all of them in one go. I would have paid good money to see his reaction but unfortunately we'll never know how he took it. I imagine not very well and the thought of the aftermath kept me chuckling for days. Shame babes.

Getting Over One by Getting Under Another

A week or two went by and I still found myself thinking about Mr Out of Proportion. Not because I was madly in love with a man I'd met once, but because I just couldn't understand how someone I'd got on so well with had just pied me off twice with no explanation. The only thing worse than knowing the harsh truth is not knowing anything at all, it makes you think up a million different things most of which put yourself at the centre of the blame. It's because I'm fat, maybe I'm shit at sex, he's judging me because I live in a council flat, and so on and so on.

I then remembered the saying "the best way to get over one man is to get under another" and that is what I set out to do. It was during this mission that I realised modern day technology has made men completely disposable, no matter how well you get on with one there's another one who can hold a decent conversation just a Tinder swipe away.

Mr PPS sent me a message saying "so you're hot, how are you?" and from there we were chatting solidly for a few weeks. He seemed funny, thoughtful, and had pretty decent chat so I thought I was onto a winner. He mentioned going to the gym a lot, being a bank manager and said he was 6'2" so I had high hopes for the bod, a decent wage and a suitably large penis. He also had a very similar dysfunctional home life to myself. He showed a lot of interest in me and appreciated the ambition I portrayed for my career which I liked a lot, and had the right balance of cheeky and gentleman. Despite all this though, I still couldn't quite place him. I wasn't sure whether he was a lad or a bit geeky. I could tell he wasn't a knobhead though so that was good.

He lived about an hour away and as we'd started talking around Christmas time we made plans for me to go and stay with him in January. As the days went on, a positive was added to our list of 'reasons to visit' every day. Naturally everything on this list was edible because nothing wins me over more than food and gin, so we'd planned Turkish delight, cake, praline chocolates, and everything else that you probably shouldn't eat when you're planning on being naked in front of someone.

We followed each other on Instagram and added each other on Snapchat so we knew what the other looked like, and on one night out I drunk dialled him but he couldn't hear me despite me being able to remember the relief of him having a normal voice. Phone calls weren't made during sober time so we were still one step behind Mr Out of Proportion but the mission to forget about him was going well.

As time went by and we chatted more I started to question whether he really was as funny as I thought he was, or if actually he was just a bit thick. I started to lose interest in him but put it down to the fact we just needed to see each other as texting for weeks can get tedious.

My keenness to meet him and get it over with hit its peak on the night of my work Christmas party. This keenness was aided by the four glasses of wine I downed on arrival, the bottle of table wine I stashed, the Sambuca, and the gin, but I was keen nonetheless. I'd already whetted his appetite when I was getting ready by sending him a picture of me wearing a sexy pout and my cleavage touching my chin which obviously he appreciated, and I held off until about midnight before the obligatory drunk dialling from the comfort of a toilet cubicle began.

He was sat at home and soberly entertained my drunken state for a fair while. I'm not sure how long we were talking before I told him he should drive and see me right now but my persuasion mode was kicked into high gear pretty quickly, throwing out 'YOLO' and 'what else are you going to do tonight?!'. Before he was completely sold, he had to hang up to check on his mother who had just arrived home and it was during this chat-break that I threw up absolutely everything I'd eaten and drank that day. Classy. When he called back he'd decided to take the hour drive down to see me. As he hit the road, I went in search of chewing gum and pep talks from colleagues then sat in a fried chicken shop waiting for him after everyone dispersed to the next venue.

    Mr PPS called me to tell me he was in the area and asked for directions to where I was. My direction skills are piss poor and he has no clue how to use any kind of technology so a sat nav or map app was out of the question. It took an hour of him driving around before he parked up on the other side of town and I stumbled across in the rain to locate him.

    It was about 2am by the time I rolled into his car looking like a drowned rat and probably still smelling of sick. Lucky boy, this two hour journey was well worth it wasn't it pal? Looking at his profile as he drove, he was definitely attractive. Well-dressed too, but the chat didn't give me any kind of excitement. When we pulled up to my house he got his overnight bag out of the boot of his car and we crept into the flat with hushed voices.

One touch which I did appreciate was his offering of Turkish delight. We sat on my bed and munched whilst moaning about how cold it was in my room. I then went and got my pyjamas on again, a move that apparently I will never grow out of. He got in his pants and we cuddled up whilst he started talking about shit. His shoulders were weedy and I couldn't get comfortable, and I started trying to sleep to drown out his Arnold Schwarzenegger impressions and his awkward way of telling a story which was in no way as entertaining as he clearly thought it was.

When the sleep attempt failed, I thought the only way to shut him up was to kiss him so that I did. He quickly had his hands in my pants and was fingering me like I was a 16 year old virgin. I stopped for a minute and gave it the old 'I'm not sure if this is a good idea', looking innocent but really questioning whether I could tolerate him being inside me, but obviously I continued anyway and we got down to it. The one thing I really dislike during sex, more than any weird shit possible, is when a man doesn't take my top off. Firstly, I have massive tits and it's only fair to show them some love, and secondly it makes me think they just want to get it in without seeing the gunt. Mr PPS did not take my top off which prevented me from getting in the mood completely.

And this is where you find out what PPS stands for. Getting me in the mood wasn't necessary anyway. He entered me with his smaller than average penis and I put my hands on his back as I love a scratch but he was furry rather than hairy and pimply which was quite gross. Then before I could even acknowledge the fact we were going at it, pump pump squirt and he was done. It couldn't have been any longer than two minutes. I was quite shocked as that has never happened, and I could tell he was quite embarrassed. However, my shock didn't hand me any sympathetic words to give to him but instead made me burst out laughing.

Just when I thought this whole situation couldn't get worse, he then rolled over and made me spoon him. Seriously, I was a foot shorter than him, he's just given me some horrendously bad sex and now I'm spooning him and feeling his stomach which felt like foreskin. I've never been more disappointed by a whole person in my entire life.

The next morning we both kept waking up, talking for a bit then falling back to sleep. Well, he fell asleep more than I did. I was desperate for a poo and for him to leave so spent most of the morning clenching my bum cheeks and wishing for time to go a bit quicker so he'd piss off.

He eventually left at about 11am. We had a few texts after this until the Monday when I decided I just couldn't be bothered to flog that two minute pony any longer. I didn't reply to his last text and I think from there it was mutually understood that this wasn't going to happen.

After the fail of this night I was left half-baked for weeks. I was desperate for some decent sex and so on Boxing Day I reactivated my Plenty of Fish and Tinder profiles and got the hang of this dating business with high hopes of a damn good seeing to along the way.

Groundwork January

January was always going to be about getting into the swing of this challenge. I needed to up my game and make sure it wasn't all about chirpsing for a while, getting drunk, having sex with them, then that being the end. I needed stories in all forms, not just ones that followed the same format as that wouldn't have been entertaining at all.

I thought I'd have a slow start but actually January has been quite full. I've managed six dates with five different men, and although I feel like I've learnt a lot about the male species there are also issues which I'm struggling with especially getting the second date. I'm starting to think maybe I'm shit on dates, or maybe I'm not as fit as my pictures. Or maybe it's both. Either way, the five men I've met this month definitely include some characters.

I also realised that this challenge is going to give me a whole lot of free stuff. Here's what I got this month:

- Nine gin and tonics
- Nandos

- Coffee
- Panini
- Two cocktails
- Eventful drunk sex
- First time sober sex
- First time second occasion sex
- Thrush (inevitable)

What I didn't consider going into this is how hard it would be to get over some of the major things that put me off men. I had to get rid of one because he turned my stomach with some things he did and there's been a few who may have given great chapters but I couldn't even bring myself to meet them.

Even looking at peoples dating profiles I manage to find something that puts me off. Here are a few things I've spotted which I'm struggling to overcome:

- Poor spelling and grammar
- iPad selfies (God give me strength)
- People who moan about 'not being given a chance' (pity sex?) or about what they're not looking for
- The line 'I like going out but I like staying in' is possibly the most ridiculous thing I've ever heard. If you like both of those options what is it you don't

like? The bit when you go in and out of your door? Do you have a temperamental doorframe that's known to splinter it's victims to death?
• When people just put 'Ask if you want to know more'. No one is good looking enough to warrant a complete lack of interests or personality

And pretty much everything else anyone has ever said or done on their online dating profiles.

Getting Back in the Game

When you first get your face onto an online dating site the messages come in thick and fast, like hyenas praying on fresh flesh. About 95% of these messages will come from ugly weirdos, but the other 5% are made up of people who are at least good looking enough to consider sleeping with. There are even a few people who seem relatively normal and can hold a conversation which is the most unexpected discovery of all.

      In the first week of January, I managed three dates. Seven years of no dates at all and I get three in one week. This one doesn't do things by halves. The first thing I learnt this month is that no matter how much or how little I like someone, even when I remember this is just all for the book, my stomach goes mental before a date. I'm talking shits, heaving, the works. There's just something about the pressure of entertaining that frightens the life out of me.

My first date was with a guy who was only ever going to be called Mr Warm Up. We met for drinks on a rainy Sunday evening after talking online and texting for a week. He was much better looking in real life but most of the conversation was taken up by him talking about his drunken antics including the time he took all of his clothes off in a local pub and a man stubbed out a cigarette on his penis. Or when he was hating life doing karaoke and wanted to get out of it so took all of his clothes off and straddled the bar. Or when he took all of his clothes off on New Year's Eve and lost his phone and his wallet. There's a common theme in these stories isn't there?

When he did get round to questioning me, he admitted to thinking I was a bit of a geek before we met. First strike of disappointment for him. This unearthed a problem with online dating. It's easy to see someone's photos, read their profile, text them for a bit, and make up your own mind about what kind of person they are without actually listening and paying attention to what they say, and completely overlooking what they're actually like. It's almost like creating your own fantasy of someone by putting your ideal personality with their face, only to leave you thwarted when you meet and realise that actually they're nothing how you imagined them to be - and that happy ever after you dreamed up slowly slips away.

Me and Mr Warm Up had a courtesy text post-date but never spoke again.

Date two of January was with Mr Too Keen. I wasn't that bothered when he first messaged me but he looked reasonably alright so I went with it. When we were talking he was verging more on irritating than giving me any kind of exciting feelings. I love a man with ambition but he worked in recruitment and spoke about it like he had some kind of incredible high flying job, like he was the CEO of a multimillion pound company. He'd tell me daily that "work is going really well :-)" without me asking, and rambled on about stuff that can only be described as pointless, mind-numbing shit.

Regardless of this, we made plans to meet one lunch time as our offices are fairly close together. As I stood waiting for him, I faced the direction he was coming from to see if I could spot him. After a few minutes of panicking I'd been stood up, he approached. And with him he brought the most awful walk I've ever seen. Imagine someone doing lunges, but quickly, whilst leaning forward and facing downwards. I almost asked if he was joking. Then he opened his mouth and it sounded like his balls hadn't dropped. You know when you meet someone and you're convinced they're gay? I also noticed that when I said something funny, it took him a few seconds to register before throwing his head back and howling out a bizarre laugh too. I thought I was the victim of some kind of prank with this one.

The good thing about a lunch date is that you know you only have an hour. Or rather, you only have to endure an hour before you can escape. To be fair to Mr Too Keen, this hour wasn't horrendous. We'd been to the same holiday destinations and even went to the same university so we had plenty to talk about whilst munching on paninis and drinking coffee (mine had a heart on it. So obviously on a date, kill me).

It was after this date that he just became too much and I realised then that whether a person's behaviour is taken as creepy or cute depends entirely on the attraction levels felt by the one on the receiving end. I discovered then that he didn't have a phone which for someone who works in recruitment is just odd, and he could only use his laptop by plugging it into his television as the screen didn't work. Suddenly I had mental images of my online dating profile pictures on his big screen as he touched himself in the dark. God help me. All of his following messages after our lunchtime rendezvous were ended with three kisses. Call me a fussy woman but after one meeting, that's excessive. He also asked me out again almost instantly, and proposed another lunchtime date with the free Starbucks voucher he'd won at work. And who said romance was dead? For the sake of the book I accepted but after a few more messages I realised that the second date may have been when he leaned in for a kiss and I physically couldn't bear the thought of it so I attempted to pie him off the only way I know how – to completely ignore him.

Unfortunately, this fella didn't quite understand that when someone first becomes distant but then ignores you completely it means they're not interested so I received a grand total of four messages before I was told 'four messages is insane, five messages means you're dead in the boot of his car so you need to shut it down'. I didn't quite fancy being murdered so replied with a half-arsed excuse about not being interested in dating at the moment and wished him luck on his quest. He replied politely (course he did) and I thought that would be the end of that until he messaged me again a few weeks later saying I'd 'popped into his head'. I used my old school method of ignoring him again and I think this may have finally got the message through.

Date three was with a young man I can only call Mr Observant for reasons that will soon become clear. Leading up to the date we were having absolute essays of messages fired back and forth and we seemed to be on the same page about general life. Both had strong ideas about our careers, a fear of 'normal life syndrome', and he called me out on my weirdness fairly quickly but seemed to find it quite endearing. He'd recently moved to a nearby town and we arranged a Sunday day date with me leading the way as he hadn't been here before. We had called me his tour guide and I was to show him what my hometown has to offer, but when it came to planning the day I realised I didn't have a fucking clue what actually was on offer apart from food and booze. So when I turned up at the train station to collect him I announced we'd be going to the local museum. He looked dubious to say the least.

The thing about living in a fairly small town with not a lot to offer is that the museum will always be quiet and there really won't be much to see. As we strolled around in the silence looking at bits of shit it was awkward to say the least. It was quite clear that we were an odd pairing, him a fairly short but not your stereotypical black man from Luton, me dressed in eBay's finest vintage trying and failing to make some kind of educated conversation about the ancestry of shrapnel and biscuit tins. We even followed the story of some old king or something on this massive tapestry for about half an hour. Him genuinely interested, me thinking of food and pointing out that whoever made it clearly wasn't very good because all their faces were weird. Looking back, I realise now that I gave up on the enthusiasm and trying to impress him about 0.5 seconds after entering the museum. A terrible date choice on my part.

    After the museum we hit Nandos for lunch as much had been said about how much I love it. He paid which was nice, but he had me guessing about that right up to the last minute so I'd started sweating slightly when I thought about the direness of my bank balance. When our food came the conversation was arguably forced. We started talking about fitness as I'd recently joined a gym and he used to be a personal trainer. Then, for reasons I still can't understand I told him why I no longer drink coke. It's because when I was in Ibiza I drank so much of it that whenever I did an alcohol-induced sick (every morning) it was coming out black. I told him this while he was eating. And had a glass of coke. At least I didn't tell him I had the shits all week which was also black and watery, so he should be grateful for that one. His face said it all, I'd just put the nail in the coffin for us and I came to terms with the fact we'd never be seeing each other again right there.

Regardless of my poor form, once lunch was over Mr Observant still suggested going for a coffee. I paid, and as I walked over to the table I caught my bag on the back of someone's chair and almost spilt two lattes all over the place. This was not my smoothest day, and sometimes being a woman who doesn't have her shit together is so obvious it's almost uncomfortable to live in my own skin.

When we left Mr Observant made the statement that gave him his name. Strolling back to the train station he said "you're quite gobby aren't you? I sussed it out within about 10 minutes of meeting you". Now maybe it's just me, but I'm not sure that is a compliment. Maybe he suggested coffee just to make sure, and to see if I could redeem myself after the absolute disaster of the whole day. Me shouting "oh fucking hell" as the coffees nearly went over almost certainly helped him to make his mind up on this one.

His train wasn't due for a while and he then suggested going for a drink. I think loitering on his own was only marginally worse than spending another half an hour with me but I accepted all the same as I was gagging for a gin and tonic after the day I'd just been through. Big screens filled all corners of the pub and captivated his attention so the conversation was completely given up on until he asked what my friends are like. "Gobby" I simply replied defeated.

As he went to leave he headed straight in the direction of the station without a glance back. "Bye then" I said, arms wide for the obligatory hug. Why I did this I'll never know. Too fucking nice for my own good I am. I also sent the 'hope you got home alright' text an hour or two later to which he casually replied. Surprisingly I never heard from him again after that.

Another Successful Weekend of Being a Player

Date four of January came in the form of a Geordie I'll call Mr Lips. Honestly, they were enormous. We met on a Friday evening after texting and speaking on Tinder for a couple of weeks. I wasn't bothered about him at all but the nerves pre-date were ridiculous. I was shitting through the eye of a needle all day, such a lady. I think part of me realised that this was the first weekend drinking date and I still hadn't had sex yet this year so the stakes were high.

      He texted me before we met to finalise plans and told me he was "really looking forward to it!" I wasn't particularly but for the sake of the book I persevered. I met him at the train station and we went for drinks in a local busy bar. I noticed quickly that he was a very awkward human being and his facial expressions didn't quite match his pictures. He had bulgy eyes, frequently flicked his tongue out to moisten the absolute sausages attached to his gob, and was generally a bit gangly but the conversation wasn't too much of a hard task and as my stomach was in too much of a state to eat dinner I managed to get quite drunk fairly quickly.

Mr Lips was a very generous man. A gentleman, some may say and he clearly felt a bit uncomfortable when I insisted on paying for a few of the rounds. I am a feminist and a strong believer in equality, I don't want men to treat me like a princess and I like to pay my way. I realise now that some men feel emasculated by this but it's tough. I'm all for the freebies during this challenge but I'm not a cunt.

When we left the first bar, Mr Lips clearly felt like this was going very well. I was having a reasonably good time but that's mainly because I fucking love gin and I was full of it to the eyeballs. It was raining and luckily I'd brought an umbrella which Mr Lips held over me whilst placing his hand on the small of my back. We then went for cocktails in another bar and it became apparent that his awkwardness didn't ease off with a few bevvies in him. If anything, it got worse. One of the barmen asked me a few times if I was being served whilst winking and giving me the eye, and Mr Lips proclaimed sulkily "well he clearly fancies you".

Maybe he does Mr Lips, grow a personality and someone might fancy you too. We sat and spoke about films and I told him I wasn't really interested in films unless someone broke out in song halfway through like my all-time favourite Sister Act 2. This probably isn't something that people find that attractive as apparently everyone loves films but we all know I've got no filter and I'm not very good at pretending to have the same hobbies and interests as someone else to impress them.

    After this we went to go to another bar but it was shut. I then remembered my friends were out in the bar next door and without giving him much choice, I dragged Mr Lips over to meet them for a laugh. Poor sod. He handled it quite well though and they didn't give him too much of a grilling so that was nice. As we walked to our final destination he saw it time to lean in for a kiss. It was alright, but I think we knew from there that this evening only had one outcome. I was getting the first D of 2014. In the last bar we got a drink each before realising there was no other person in there. "You can come back to mine if you want" he said. "Alright, now?" I said before downing my drink. Someone's keen.

    In the taxi Mr Lips put his arm around me and said with an astounded tone "I've never gone home with someone on the first date before".

There's probably a reason for that but hey, I'm always here to help. So charitable I am. We got back to his, made small talk as he put some music on and I text all my friends saying "I'm at his. SOMEONE GETTIN' LAAAID". I then led the way to his bedroom and we started what could only be described as a very eventful sex session. Although fairly quiet and gentlemanly in public, Mr Lips gave me a serious beasting in the bedroom. It was outrageous, we were going for over an hour, and at one very questionable point he shoved his finger up my arse and called me a 'bad bad girl'. I didn't enjoy this very much and would strongly advise all men never to do this on the first time you meet someone, but the rest of it was alright from what I can remember.

When we woke up the next morning he was ready to go for another round. I was hanging, felt a bit sick and looked and smelt like death but let him continue all the same. He obviously sensed my reluctance as when he entered me he said "I feel like I'm raping you". I wasn't too bothered and certainly wasn't going to call the police but seeing his face in the cold light of day did not make me feel very well at all. Maybe it's just the angle I thought. Maybe it's what happens when he's hungover. Maybe it's the lighting of the sun that's making his eyes seem even more bulgy and his lips even more enormous. I closed my eyes and thought of England as they say and just as he was falling back to sleep after trying and failing to spoon me (casual shuffle to the edge on my part) I asked if he'd mind taking me home. It was only 9.30am but lying in our juices in his uncomfortable bed with the sun shining in through the blinds forced me to call time.

After Mr Lips dropped me home that morning, date five of January picked me up later that very same evening.

The fifth and final date of January was with Mr Pen Pal, named so because we were texting for a month before finally meeting. He was one of the first people to message me when I set up my Plenty of Fish profile and he was probably my favourite one. Possibly because he seemed like a bit of a bellend and I'd heard bad things about him so naturally I wanted to play him good and make him fall in love with me. I should have known after trying to pin him down for a month that wasn't going to happen. My bad. When we first started talking we worked out our mutual friends and he forgot to mention the fact he'd not only chatted one of my best friends up for a while but had aggressively pinned another one up against a wall and stuck his tongue in her mouth. All while he was still with his previous girlfriend. Selective memory or what? He also lied about the fact he had a child on his profile and rather than mentioning it, sent me a video of them singing together. Luckily I'd already been told about this by my friends so it wasn't too much of a shock but I'm sure there are better ways of telling people you've got a kid, like not lying on your dating profile for instance.

He was filthy quite early on so was probably just looking to stick his dick in a few women rather than find a meaningful relationship but I'm an animal so of course I enjoyed it very much. I especially enjoyed showing his dirty messages to my friends and work colleagues and watching them recoil in horror when he graphically described what he was going to do to me. We had two dates planned before we finally met, the first cancelled because he forgot to mention he wouldn't be ready until about 9pm which quite frankly is far too late during the week, and the second cancelled because I didn't hear from him and apparently he was fed up of texting me first and chasing me every day. Which to be fair he did, but a player doesn't chase does she?

When we finally met, he picked me and my hangover up from my council flat on the Saturday after the Friday spent with Mr Lips. At the beginning of this challenge I really didn't want people to see where I lived, not because I'm a snob but because I know what people think and people and their judgements can fuck off. This one had also painted himself out to be a bit of a flashy bastard and it's those exact types that I didn't want to reveal my living circumstances to. He'd told me he spent £600 on a pair of trainers and spoke about his brands even though his clothes to me looked like they could have come fresh from Primark.

    Mr Pen Pal was very insistent on collecting me and wouldn't tell me where we were going beforehand so I had no choice but to let him. He drove us to a pub that was 74 miles away (it probably wasn't that far but I have no concept of geography or distance) and had about two people in it. It wasn't even a particularly nice establishment so why he felt the need to drive all the way there was beyond me but I can only imagine he didn't want to be spotted by anyone. What a great way to make a girl feel good. On the way there he was telling me about how his mate had got someone pregnant and how they had dodgy acquaintances who can 'sort people out', with his mate threatening to get them to kill her and/or her baby. What lovely people you surround yourself with sir, I feel ever so safe in the middle of nowhere with you.

The date was completely underwhelming. Whilst sat in this quiet, average pub in the middle of nowhere Mr Pen Pal spent the whole time on his phone. I say 'whole time' like we made an evening of it but actually I had two drinks and he had one soft drink because he was driving. The conversation in person compared to how we spoke via text was distinctly average and I decided quite quickly that I wouldn't be having sex with him that evening despite how much of a good story it would have been to have got through two in one weekend. Somehow the conversation got onto girls who put out on the first date and for some reason I found myself saying "I'd never do that, it's terrible". I'd definitely done it the night before, excuse me while I lol. I even found myself thinking "why are you saying this?" but my mouth just carried on, like it was a separate part of my body that was trying to induce some humour into this poor date.

When he dropped me off I wasn't really sure what I was meant to do as after all the build-up the evening had been a massive letdown. So I went for a hug. Apparently that's not a cool thing to do but I wasn't going to kiss him and I think a high five would have been even worse. I sent him a post-date courtesy text and he didn't reply, yet despite how badly the evening had gone I was still pissed off. A whole month of groundwork for THAT. More thoughts about how I'm not as fit in real life as I am in my pictures flooded my brain as I simply couldn't understand how he'd gone from chasing me for a month to throwing a pie immediately after meeting me. After 24 hours of sulking I got over it and realised that he's just a massive bellend who I didn't want to see again or have sex with anyway. And that was the limp end of Mr Pen Pal.

The next day, the Sunday of the same weekend, Mr Lips text me asking if I fancied going round to his to watch a DVD. I declined because I was tired and was glad of it the next day when I discovered that 'watch a DVD' was an internationally recognised phrase for 'have sex'. How had I managed to go 24 years without anyone inviting me round to watch a DVD before!? I'm so inexperienced, what is wrong with me. At the time of him asking I suggested Tuesday and went over with a freshly groomed vagina and the frightening knowledge that I was about to have second occasion and sober sex in the space of one night.

I made him watch Pitch Perfect and whilst I was thoroughly enjoying it I still wasn't sure at what point of a 'watch a DVD' evening the sex commenced. Because of this, I made no plays for it until the very end and made him sit through the whole film. There was one part where he kissed me but I brushed it off and he also kept kissing the top of my head with his massive lips every time I readjusted which made me cringe so in the end I stopped moving and lost all use of my left arm. Once the credits started running we got down to business. He lived in his own flat and had a lovely big corner sofa but stopped during the kissing and groping to say "there's not much room on here". There was loads of room on there, I really wanted to be adventurous and have sex on the sofa but clearly he had a fear of spilling semen on the upholstery so we trailed off to the bedroom and started getting down to it fairly quickly. Right after he entered me he confirmed what I already suspected. He doesn't talk about sex unless he's actually having it. He entered me and said "we broke my bed on Friday". That's quite funny, why wouldn't you tell me that the next day?

  The sober sex with Mr Lips was completely vanilla. In, out, done. I very nearly came and got the shaking legs thing going on but he was done before I reached climax which I wasn't too bothered about as I had completed the sober sex and second occasion sex challenge and was starting to finally feel like an experienced shagger. What an achievement.

We continued to text through the week and arranged date three, dinner, for the week after. During the days leading up to it I really didn't want to go. I'd had the click and the thought of him was making me feel sick. Unfortunately, once the click is done and they move over into repulsion it's impossible to get back onto tolerable ground. I still went anyway but had text him with a little white lie before we met saying I was on my period so I didn't have to have sex with him again. When he picked me up he said "I realised earlier I should have booked somewhere. I called around and have managed to get us in one place; apparently it's a bit shit". So pleased I came mate, cheers.

    To say the conversation was forced is an understatement. I'd ask a question, he'd answer it, then silence. Just over and over again. When we got to our destination he was on edge the whole time as he'd decided to take me to a restaurant in the town where he works as a teacher and really didn't want to see any of his students of fellow staff-members. As you can imagine this made the evening even more awkward and after three gin and tonics I couldn't be bothered to make conversation with him anymore so when I wasn't in the toilet texting my friends saying I wanted to go home I sat in silence at the table. When our food came I didn't take my eyes off my plate because I couldn't bear the thought of watching his big old lips eat a lasagne. Afterwards I asked how his dinner was. His reply was "shit". Straight to the point, one word summed up not only his dinner but the entire evening. When we left it was only about 8pm and he suggested going back to his, no doubt in the hope of a thank you blowjob for dinner but I politely declined claiming I was tired. To be fair I was tired, tired of him. He drove me home, again in silence, and I gave him a kiss out of courtesy before getting out of the car. When I got in I heaved. Genuinely, more than once, I heaved at the thought of kissing him. I made up my mind there and then that I definitely would not be seeing him again.

    I'm not very good at ending things with people so I handled the sacking off in the usual cruel way. I ignored him. I ignored his text and I continued to ignore his eight Snapchats before finally blocking him and never hearing from him again. It was during these eight Snapchats that I realised who he looked like. Labour party leader Ed Miliband. The realisation hit me like a tonne of bricks and I have never felt so unclean in my life. I wanted to bleach myself inside and out, and it's something I will probably never forget for the rest of my life for all the wrong reasons.

DISCLAIMER: The next few chapters aren't very funny I'm afraid. In fact, they're a bit shit. Not in a "fuck this, what a waste of money" way, more in a "well this was a very unfortunate incident and I am not lolling anymore *sad face*" way. I debated adding some humour but actually, the situation wasn't very funny at all so I've kept it all sad and raw and that. If you don't fancy it, I won't be offended if you skip forward a few chapters. If you do continue, I promise it gets funny again afterwards like an amazing dessert after a proper disappointing dinner.

The One Who Could Have Ended the Book

"Someday you'll meet a man and he'll sweep you off your feet and promise you the world. You just punch that lying bastard and run as fast as you can."

"SO SOON?!" I hear you weep? Yep. For all my gabbing about how I was in 'business-only' mode and how human beings are awful to each other, I caught the dreaded fucking feels in February. One month into this sodding challenge, what a failure. However, if you're intelligent enough to read the signs here and you can already tell that it didn't work out – congratulations you are correct. Mr Disappointment lasted a grand total of nine weeks before the mist of infatuation wore off and I bullet-proofed my life of his poison. In this chapter I'll tell you the tale, with special 'hindsight' boxes outlining the red flags I failed to spot from the very beginning. If you want to play along and spot them for yourself, please feel free to skip these boxes and return to them later to check your answers.

On February 5th Mr Disappointment strolled into my Plenty of Fish world with the opening line 'Your face makes my penis twitch'. Not the most gentlemanly use of words but we know how filthy I am so of course I loved it. Our messages were regular, we got on ridiculously well, and he seemed perfect. His profile was written in a genuine manner and his carefully selected pictures made him seem like a truly decent young man; a rare kind, especially in the realm of online dating. Within days of online talk we were onto texting constantly and it was little over a week before the phone calls started. I say the phone calls started, it was me calling him at his request as he hadn't paid his phone bill and couldn't ring out (Hindsight 1.).

> **Hindsight 1.** How in fuck's name are you able to text all day if you haven't paid your bill? Phone companies do not cut off your ability to make calls but think "Oh it's alright, we'll let him onto the POF app and text still because a man needs to chirpse". I later found out that actually he's on pay as you go and had 100 minutes from every top up that he didn't fancy using on me.

We got on even better on the phone and after one weekend of calls I went into work and declared "I have caught feelings. This one is not going to be a chapter." I was smitten with someone

I'd never met, and rightfully so as he was wonderful. In my head the book had been put to bed and I felt fine about it. It was like I'd forgotten who I was, with my friends all very confused about this soppy twat I'd suddenly become. We talked about things most of our friends didn't even know about us in regards to home life, and our full relationship histories were laid bare almost immediately (Hindsight 2.).

> **Hindsight 2.** Turns out there's a very good reason why some people pry on your relationship history so early on, and that is because they like to use it against you later on when they start acting like a cock. "You're ruining this because of how you've been treated in the past". Nope, you're ruining it because you're a fucking bellend.

In between phone calls I received texts saying he missed me and I would wake up to lovely messages every morning telling me he was thinking about me. For the first time in my life someone was being outrageously slushy and it didn't make my skin crawl. I had made a break-through. I put it down to the fact that he was also quite often filthy with it and thought that he was just the perfect combination of gentleman and animal. We quickly got into a routine where I'd wake up to his messages and I'd call him at 7.30 every morning to wake him up. A harder task than you'd think as his phone had no sound so he'd sleep with his easily removed headphones in and I'd often be calling for half an hour as my guilty conscience wouldn't let me give up.

He told me his first girlfriend broke up with him five months before they were due to get married as she didn't love him anymore, and his more recent ex-girlfriend just didn't make the effort to see him and was in bed with another man the following week (Hindsight 3.). This poor guy, being so mistreated in the past. We're so similar, I thought.

> **Hindsight 3.** Surely no one can be that much of a cunt that they make no effort to see their boyfriend of two years when they're doing the long-distance thing. I haven't met or spoken to this woman who managed to put up with him for so long but I can confidently say that there's no way this is why they broke up. I know this due to seeing straight through him and from copious amounts of social media stalking of her, naturally.

On Tuesday 18th February, less than two weeks after he sent the first message, we had a phone chat planned again for the sixth evening in a row. Unfortunately my mum was rushed into hospital (don't worry, she's fine) so the chat was put off. But as he had a week off and didn't have to be up early, I called him when I got in anyway. I'd already told my manager I wouldn't be in work the next day so a quick chat at 2am with Mr Disappointment didn't seem unreasonable when neither of us had to be up at the crack of dawn. Seven and a half hours later we fell asleep on the phone together after the longest 'quick chat' of my life. We told each other every single thing about ourselves, including how many people we'd slept with and people we'd already met off POF. He liked to talk about girls he'd seen or pulled in the past a lot, claiming to be an open book and he even put an 'honesty policy' in place (Hindsight 4.).

Talking about other girls was something that came into conversation often and I did feel jealous. I brushed it off regularly and I convinced myself that actually it was nice to be honest, and why wouldn't he be when there's an honesty policy in place? He told me he'd slept with over 50 girls and was ashamed of it, and said the last time he'd had sex was in early December with a girl he met on POF. This later changed to Boxing Day as he'd forgotten he shagged one Christmas Eve and one two days later whilst in his home town for Christmas. I can't even flag this up as a hindsight point as I found it strange at the time that he'd 'forgotten' two girls, especially when he said "I couldn't even tell you how many girls I slept with since breaking up with my ex" which according to his previous stories would have only been a duration of a month. No one forgets how many people they've slept with in a month when they're holding down a full-time job. I did ask if he was planning on getting checked out after all these women as he'd already told me he refused to wear condoms but insisted he was clean and knew that because the one time he did have chlamydia he couldn't sustain an erection.

> **Hindsight 4.** I know. What kind of mug falls for an 'honesty policy'? Oh yeah, ME. That's basically like saying 'I'm a compulsive liar but you'll believe everything I tell you because I said I'm honest'. Cheers then. Also, if you think you want to hear every sex story a potential love interest has – trust me, you really don't. You really shouldn't continue to listen if they tell you they're on POF while you're on the phone to them either.

That day we spent a further three hours talking during dinner time, and another two hours before bed. In 24 hours we'd spent 12 and a half of them on the phone and yet we still found things to talk about. In between the sex stories and what I now know to be bullshit, he was attentive, interested, and keen. He'd say things like "if we get on this well in person I can already see a future for us. I'm excited to see where this goes". Despite being off work for a week, he was unable to do anything or go back to his hometown to visit family as his card had been cloned by someone in Yorkshire and his bank account completely cleared out, so he was on the end of the phone all evening and texting me all day during work. The contact was constant and I could feel myself falling hard for someone I'd never even met. I wasn't scared of how I felt about him which is probably the scary thing in itself; I trusted him completely and would tell him all about the conversations I'd had with people about him and how he'd melted the ice queen. He enjoyed it and seemed proud of the fact he'd brought out another side of me, always asking what I'd said to people and thriving off the lovely things I'd said to others about him, and told me he'd told all of his friends, housemates, colleagues and his mum about me. The one thing I didn't tell him during these early stages was that I'd also shown all of these people, including every friend I have and my work colleagues, the picture of his penis he'd sent me. There are some things that don't need sharing. I did tell him I'd shown my friends a bit later on and to say he was upset is an understatement.

    We arranged to meet on Tuesday 25th February as he had the Wednesday and Thursday off work and it was his payday, so after the card cloning nightmare he'd finally have some money. He lived a 30 minute train journey away and came down from work to meet me for drinks with the intention of getting the last train home at 11pm. The night before we met we scheduled in a FaceTime session for a chat but on his way home he told me his housemate's girlfriend had text him to say they were getting drunk. He insisted, of his own accord, that he wouldn't be getting involved however I then didn't hear from him until 11pm that night. He called absolutely hammered to tell me the same housemate's girlfriend was pestering him for a threesome. I proceeded to call my friend in tears after waiting all night for him to reply to my message and to be faced with that instead. I claimed this whole situation to be too stressful and how I was pissed off that he would likely be hungover for our date (Hindsight 5.).

> **Hindsight 5.** At face value, me crying over this probably seems petty. However now I think that my tears were actually a product of the build-up from red flags I'd previously ignored. I probably should have known then that he was a fucking idiot but instead I continued, like the apparent moron I am.

On the way to meet him I was nervous but excited for the first time this year. As I approached him in the bar he was waiting for me he stood up and gave me a massive hug. We didn't look like we were on our first date and it didn't feel like we were either as we already knew everything there was to know about each other. As we chatted and eased into each other's real life company there was no level of disappointment from me at all. He seemed just as wonderful as he had during the late night phone chats and we spent the evening laughing through non-stop conversation and a lot of alcohol.

When we moved onto the next bar he decided he really didn't want to go home at 11 and started ringing round hotels for him to stay at. I'd already made it quite clear before the meeting that I wouldn't be sleeping with him on our first date as Mr Out of Proportion had already pied me off immediately after the sex and that wasn't a feeling I wished to replicate any time soon. So I reminded him (and myself) that if he did get a hotel, I wouldn't be staying there with him. As a preventative method, I didn't shave any part of my body so I certainly wouldn't have wanted to get it out after a few drinks. Body hair – my favourite form of contraception. Despite the no sex rule, it was in this second bar that we started kissing. It got a bit heated and at one point he couldn't stand up for a while due to his massive erection which, I may or may not have felt through his trousers. Luckily we were tucked away in a corner and no one could see us, although I don't think either of us would have cared too much if they could. There were no hotel rooms available (Hindsight 6.) so he told me I had to stay out with him until the early hours and he'd get the first train home at 6am.

> **Hindsight 6.** Looking at the hotels he called and how dead town was that night, there is no chance none of them had any rooms available. Thinking about it now, I'm fairly certain that actually he didn't dial any of them but instead had a little chat with himself.

  Mr Disappointment decided he wanted to dance so I took him to the same bar as I'd taken Mr Lips only to discover it was completely empty and no dancing would be taking place. The way he conversed with the bar staff made me fancy him so much more in comparison to Old No Personality during the previous visit. He was charming and outgoing, confident without being cocky, and I loved it. After this we went to another place that would be open until the early hours but I hate it there at the best of times and this was a student night that I did not want to be part of. We lasted about half an hour before I realised the last train was long gone and the thought of putting up with that venue for another three hours made me want to die. I told him I was taking him home for a spoon but reminded him that absolutely no sex would be happening whatsoever. He enthusiastically agreed and promised to respect my wishes as we left.

Before heading home we went and got food, and in my drunken state I was slouched across the table noshing a burger like I'd never eaten before. Had I been with any other man I would have known this was completely unacceptable but with Mr Disappointment it felt like I'd known him forever. I was already too comfortable too soon, and he laughed at me rather than telling me how disgusting I was which reinforced my feelings as I felt like he accepted me in a way no other man ever would.

When we got home we got into bed and kissed and chatted before spooning and falling asleep. He didn't try for the sex which I was pleased about as it showed that, despite a lot of alcohol, he still played by my rules. I was in complete bliss finally falling asleep in the arms of the man my life had suddenly revolved around for the last three weeks. The next morning we agreed he'd stay in my bed while I went to work and he'd meet me in town at lunch time. We'd already made plans for him to come down that day so spending another day with him didn't seem too full on. As I got ready for work he playfully pulled me back into bed with him and tried to convince me not to leave in between kisses and cuddles. I was ten minutes late to work but my manager let me off once I'd given him the full run-down of the night's events. Everyone was in shock that I'd managed to find someone so great online and was happy for me as I went on and on about him all day whilst feeling like hell due to my hangover and lack of sleep.

    Mr Disappointment met me in town at lunch time as arranged, wearing the same clothes he'd come in the night before but with the recent addition of my hoody (which I then never saw again because he stole it). We went for a big fry up where I witnessed the weird way he eats a fried egg, which apparently no other woman has ever been privileged enough to have seen so early on. Lucky me. He wasn't one for hand holding or any signs of affection so we didn't kiss during the day at all but he did give me a big hug outside my work before wandering around town for four hours while I finished work. Him staying again that night had been hinted at and I spent all afternoon dreading the sex we'd inevitably be having. It's unlike me to not want to get it in so I put it down to being horrendously tired as I discussed this with everyone, asking them how I could muster up the enthusiasm for a session. As I do love sex and humour is my main tool, I don't think anyone around me quite understood the dread I was feeling for it so was told to crack on and man up several times. Despite all advice I still didn't want it at all, yet when we met after work and he asked "it is ok for me to stay isn't it?" to which I said yes because I still didn't want him to go home. I said I wouldn't be putting out again to see how he took it, but his reaction was "there's no way I could go another night without it". No choice for me there then (Hindsight 7.).

> **Hindsight 7.** If something inside says you don't want to have sex and they tell you you've got no choice, don't have sex with them. Unless you're me or stupid.

As I was a shell of a human being we agreed to get a takeaway and eat at home. I did tell him that this came with one compromise – he'd have to meet my mum as I couldn't sneak him into my bedroom without introducing them. My mum was thrilled about this. She'd heard all about him and it was the first time I'd taken a boy home so she could hardly contain herself, especially as I later found out her and my brother were convinced I was a raging lesbian.

He bought food for the three of us and it was around this time he started mentioning how he'd spent so much money in the time he'd visited. I wasn't sure what he wanted me to do about it as I was days away from payday and had nothing to offer so I kept quiet as money talk makes me feel uncomfortable at the best of times. Plus I had spent my last £100 on drinks the night before and footed the bill for lunch so it wasn't like I'd sat back and allowed him to fund me. When we got home we sat eating while Mr Disappointment and mum got to know each other and I sat in silence trying not to fall asleep into a plate of chips. I couldn't stop thinking about the fact I still had to shave my fanny and probably have sex with so little desire to do so when all I wanted to do was sleep. I showered and shaved regardless, like a man dolling himself up for the electric chair, and had no problem with putting my pyjamas on and letting him see my naked face. He told me that was just how he wanted me before affectionately blow drying my hair as I internally psyched myself up for the evenings events.

When we got into bed it wasn't long before he tried it on. At first I resisted, offering the morning instead and asking if I could just go to sleep but he rolled out of the spoon and sighed in a big, huffy strop. My guilty conscience came into play here. His silence and strop made me think that after all the money and time he'd spent on the visit I should have sex with him, so I did (Hindsight 8.).

> **Hindsight 8.** Yes, I know. Sex is not a trade for someone's time or money. Ladies reading this please do not follow in my footsteps. Just because a man willingly spends money on your dates it does not mean that you owe him anything, especially access to your vagina.

The sex was absolutely ridiculous and I'm not sure if I mean that in a good way. He was throwing me into all kinds of positions and being quite rough, despite knowing my fragile state, so at the beginning I pretty much just laid there and took it in shock at what was happening. I did eventually start getting into it and almost enjoyed it but that wasn't until after he asked me to suck his cock. I declined, he whined, but then got into a safe and steady missionary position to finish the job. He came, I didn't unsurprisingly, and while he was still on top of and inside me he checked his phone to see who text him during the sex. Seriously. Apparently it was his male friend but I wouldn't be overly surprised if it was another bird he was replying to in that post-sex state.

Afterwards we went for a cigarette and I felt odd in a way I can't explain. I wasn't happy; I was quiet and almost felt a bit confused at the whole situation that had just happened. He could tell as well as he asked me multiple times if I was alright.

The next morning was completely different to how the previous morning had been. There was no waking up with me and playing around, instead he rolled to the other side of the bed and put his head under the pillow and when I left he didn't so much as flinch. We had a few texts when he woke up, with him asking when my mum would be back as he now didn't want to come and meet me for lunch again as we had arranged. When he realised he'd probably be faced with my family if he stayed in bed, he begrudgingly decided to come into town but seemed less than keen to meet me. I ended up seeing him for about ten minutes as he left late and again there were no public displays of affection at all. In fact, I don't even think there was so much as a hug when he greeted me. He also told me he hadn't bothered to make my bed as he had before, and hadn't washed up the shit he'd used. This effort decline was shockingly rapid but I put it down to us being too comfortable too quickly. He said he'd meet me again after work before he left to go back home and went off to the casino to kill some time as he'd boasted about how good he was in there and how he never lost. Mr Disappointment came out of the casino £100 down but apparently won it all back on a quick gamble in the betting shop on the way to meeting me for dinner at the end of my working day.

We had a cheap dinner in a pub before going to the train station for him to go back home. He said that he was upset he didn't make me come and soon formulated a checklist of sexual things he wanted to get through with me, asking what I had and hadn't done. As we said goodbye I grabbed him and gave him a proper kiss which he seemed slightly resistant to but continued all the same. I had told him previously I'd be waiting to hear from him and would take the hint if I didn't. He text me almost instantly after leaving me and we texted until his phone died halfway through his journey.

It was after this meeting he started calling me a 'keeno' despite knowing how much it pissed me off. I didn't like how he made it sound like I was way more into him than he was into me, but he still continued until the shit hit the fan in the next chapter and my keen-ness obviously wore off.

That weekend I was visiting a friend in Wales and he texted me on the Friday telling me he'd cashed up the tills at his work, left the money on the side and someone had taken it. He refused to tell the area manager as he was sure he'd be sacked, and he went on and on about how he'd have to replace the money but would be left with no money for food or bus fare for the rest of the month. The amount that he spoke about money was already bothering me and I wasn't sure if he was hinting for me to help him out but I kept my mouth shut, knowing better than to give money to a man I'd met on the internet.

As the weekend went on he called me a few times knowing I was with my friends and they were impressed with how keen he seemed. On the Saturday night out I ended up having to leave early after not feeling well and the next morning when I spoke to him he told me I should have called him. I wasn't really sure why I should have as he wasn't my boyfriend and as far as he was concerned we were still 'taking it slow' so I found it a bit odd that he came back with such a stereotypically nice response. I think there may have been something in it that felt insincere as I hadn't felt like that after anything nice he'd said before. It almost seemed as like he was trying to make himself look good with the nice words and calling me without asking me to call him back to not waste his minutes.

The following week he kept mentioning the money that was taken from his work, how stressed he was that he'd have to replace it, would definitely lose his job if anyone found out, and would be living on air for the next three weeks. It got to the point where I called my friends and asked if I should offer some money after how much he'd spent while he was down but we all agreed that was a ridiculous idea and I was only thinking it because of how much he was going on about it.

During one of our many phone conversations we arranged for me to go stay with him on the Friday night, a week and a half after we'd first met. He had no money due to the till saga so I said I'd make jerk chicken for him and would leave early in the morning as he had work and I was going away for a friend's birthday. The day before the visit I went and bought all the food bits for dinner and spent the evening making the sauce and marinating the chicken before packing my bag and frantically outfit planning for the following day. On the Friday, I got up early to shower and shave so I was fresh and preened, and took my chicken and overnight bag off to work whilst counting down the minutes until I could get on the train to see Mr Disappointment. He asked if I'd bought a pudding which I hadn't so my lunch hour was spent rushing around whilst on the phone to him to make sure I got what he wanted and I ended up spending a fortune on food just for one night.

As he was so skint, he couldn't afford to meet me at the train station so he directed me (poorly) to the bus stop and got me lost a few times, telling where to get off as he'd be waiting there for me. When I met him, he looked at his phone and said "you have 9 unread messages from the past week… I haven't even been on there", referring to another dating app (Hindsight 9.) before giving me a welcome hug.

> **Hindsight 9.** I don't even need to say anything here really, do I? Hi, nice to see you… Oh no.

He told me his housemate and his girlfriend were in (the one asking him for a threesome) and I panicked as I had a feeling she wouldn't like me after cockblocking her and the mate of hers she tried to set up with Mr Disappointment. However, she was actually quite nice, if slightly mental, and the four of us ended up spending the evening together while he drank their booze and I made him dinner. For such an awful person, he had an excellent way of making people give him what he wanted without them getting suspicious. He was incredibly attentive all evening, kissing me, hugging me, and pulling me onto his lap whilst telling me he's "never this soppy with anyone" and calling me "a good egg" (Hindsight 10.).

> **Hindsight 10.** He spotted my good nature far too early on which is probably why this story planned out like it did. Thought he could take advantage, however my good nature doesn't last very long when someone is taking the fucking piss.

When we finally went to bed at half 10, I was the most amount of horny I had ever been in my life and lucky for me, Mr Disappointment had already decided to make it his mission to make me come after I told him no man ever had before. I asked him for a massage which didn't last long and then he got to work on me with his mouth and fingers, attacking my clit like a genie would pop out and grant him three wishes if he rubbed it hard enough. As he prided himself on being so good in bed, I didn't ask him to change his technique when it started hurting as I knew climax was imminent. He congratulated himself heavily when it happened before giving me the best sex of my life for the next hour. I gave him the blowjob he was so desperate for and letting become the first man to come in my mouth and then swallowing it: two more ticks off his checklist. We ended up in a sweaty heap for about 30 seconds before he jumped up to shower refusing to kiss me until I brushed my teeth and rid my mouth of his juices (Hindsight 11.).

> **Hindsight 11.** It wasn't until about three months later that I realised this post-sex behaviour wasn't entirely normal. Somehow, it came up into conversation at work and I asked both men and women whether they insisted on showering immediately and if they kissed after oral. Everyone's answers were the complete opposite of what Mr Disappointment did, making me realise that if a man is lucky enough to come in your mouth, you deserve a fucking kiss for it afterwards.

As I was so unaware of the correct protocol after sober sex, I concentrated entirely on how good it had been. I didn't think about the fact he'd told me the two times his phone went off during the session had been Snapchats from the two other girls off POF he met (and apparently had no further contact with), and we cuddled and chatted for a while before attempting to sleep. I've never been in love with anyone before but thinking about this moment still makes me sad as it's probably the closest to love I have ever felt. Lying in his single bed with my blinkers on to his red flags felt almost perfect, when really I didn't even know who he was at this point at all. We tried for round two before bed but after he half-heartedly attempted to get me wet and decided it wasn't happening for me, he had a wank next to me instead (Hindsight 12.).

> **Hindsight 12.** I don't think I've spoken to anyone about this but writing it makes me think this might not be a normal thing either.

The heating in his house was on constantly and as his room wasn't even big enough to swing a cat in, hence the single bed we were sharing, I did not sleep well at all. I woke up at one point and pressed his phone button as it was closer to see what the time was. I saw a Facebook message from a girl he'd met on a night out a few weeks previously. Panicking, I got up for a 5am cigarette to think things through but decided that if it was only on Facebook rather than texting it can't mean anything and they surely can't talk that often. He later confirmed this without me mentioning it when he looked at his phone and said "what the fuck" before telling me all about it, unaware I'd already seen the messages and had drawn that exact conclusion.

We got the bus together in the morning at around 8am so he'd be in work on time and I'd have a few hours to chill at home before going away for the night with my friends, kissing me once as we said goodbye. Like the last time we saw each other, he text me first fairly soon afterwards to check I was safely on my way home and we continued to speak constantly all weekend.

It was on the following Tuesday that trouble in paradise struck.

When the Shit Hit the Fan

As I mentioned previously, the sound on Mr Disappointment's phone didn't work. Because of this, he had his earphones in all the time and would always speak to me this way too. On the Tuesday after I visited with chicken, this unique way of him using the phone got him into hot water and caused our first fallout.

One of his housemates was a man in his 50s from Holland and with the language barrier came quite a bit of confusion and misunderstanding. Mr Disappointment was on the phone to me with this housemate in the same room. Whilst asking me questions, the housemate didn't realise I was a part of the conversation and kept answering Mr Disappointment instead. At first we found this hilarious; he kept asking a question and saying my name with the housemate unaware of what was happening and continuing to talk. Mr Disappointment then brought me up. They spoke about me for a few exchanges before the housemate then asked another question which I didn't hear. Mr Disappointment laughed and said "well this is awkward, I'm actually on the phone to Reading chick now" (the nickname that replaced my actual name). I asked him what had been said and he replied "nothing babe" whilst still laughing. Turns out the housemate had asked how it was going with the other girls from POF. He'd only lived there a few weeks and according to Mr Disappointment no one else had been over in the time we'd been talking.

    I went quiet and my barriers instantly went straight back up. Earlier in the day he'd put a meme picture about sluts in his hometown on Facebook and someone had commented saying that it was rich coming from him. He'd replied with "I am a slut, but a classy one!" which only added to my angst about being taken for a ride. We weren't in a relationship but the amount we talked and the way we'd spent nights together when we'd seen each other made it feel like it was heading that way quickly. He'd also said a few times that he was no longer using POF (without me asking) so if he was still talking to people on there that was a breach of his own honesty policy which I didn't feel very happy about. He said that the Hollander had overheard him and another housemate talking about the girls. Having met the guy apparently asking this question, I don't believe he would have indulged in that kind of 'girls of POF past' conversation with them, or had the mental capacity to casually overhear and understand another conversation.

I couldn't have a normal conversation with him after that, so I told him I was going to which he replied "fine, bye" before hanging up as if I was being unreasonable. He then text me saying "Seriously, what's wrong with you?" to which I stated the obvious. I received no reply and no nice text to wake up to, but I did see his Facebook status. "Women… One of life's great mysteries" Fucking moron.

I decided I had to bite the bullet and call him to wake him up, which took ages as usual, and when he finally answered nothing about the night before was mentioned and we just carried on as normal. When we spoke later in the evening he told me if I have a problem I have to speak to him on the phone about it because texting annoyed him. I had to play by his rules so to not upset him despite talking openly on the phone about issues not coming naturally to me.

For the rest of the week we didn't speak as much as we had before. On one evening, he disappeared for hours without getting in contact and after my failed attempts at calling him something made me look to see if he'd been on POF. He had. After all of his insisting he never went on it anymore, he'd been online that day and his profile headline had changed since we'd met. When he did eventually contact me I didn't mention it because I couldn't be bothered for another argument and we'd already planned for me to go down that weekend so I thought it best to see how it was when I saw him instead.

  One thing I started noticing in the build-up to me seeing him was how he was more excited about what we'd be eating than seeing me. He was still skint so the weekend would be funded by me again, and we'd planned for me to stay the Friday and Saturday night despite him working all weekend. On the day I was due to go down, I was full of dread. There were things about him that were bothering me including him clearly speaking to other girls on the side. I spent my lunch break with some colleagues where I moaned constantly about the fact he had no hobbies or interests, no TV, no laptop, and no friends where he lived. I didn't even exaggerate what I said about him for everyone to tell me they thought he sounded like a loser and I knew they were right. No hobbies or interests may sound like a fussy thing to be bothered about, but he didn't ever seem to want to do anything apart from sit in. He never went out, had no interest in new music, films, or TV, had literally nothing in his life apart from work, watching football on his phone, and sleep. As someone with a hectic social life, a full time job, working on a part time degree, and having done a fair amount of volunteering for charity the previous year I like people who make the most of life and he certainly wasn't one of them.

When I went down on the Friday after work, we went food shopping for the weekend's meals and alcohol. As he was filling up the basket I ended up spending about £50 on things we were never going to eat. Seemingly, I was stocking his cupboards for him. When we got back to his we had a few drinks and nachos before the housemate from Holland came in and asked if we were 'going steady' now we'd spent a few evenings together. Mr Disappointed replied quickly with "no" then when he was pushed to answer the housemate with what we were, he said "a bit more than just friends". All housemates dispersed and it ended up just the two of us, drinking more and dancing round the kitchen. He plugged his phone into the speakers but had no signal and said "I know how to fix this, if I go to call someone it comes back" before going onto his call history. And there it was. Second on the list, timed right before he called me when I got off the train, was 'Zoe POF'. Just like Tuesday, I froze up and tried to act like I was alright. Tried and failed, he again asked me a million times what was wrong with me, obviously knowing I'd just seen it.

    He eventually got me to sit down with him so he could talk to me. He asked again what was wrong and I said "well, have another look at your call history". He did and told me that she was some girl from ages before he'd spoken to me who had randomly called him out of the blue. He then said "she means nothing, look I'll delete her number. I don't answer calls from numbers I don't know" after going onto WhatsApp and accidentally showing there was a conversation between them on there too, and he said "I know this in-between stage is hard while we're getting to know each other but you have to trust me or it won't work. I'm not a dickhead like the guys you've been fucked over by before". Except that he was, and he was equally as good at the chat as they were.

    When we went to bed, the sex was a bit of a nightmare. He couldn't keep it up, I was tired, and it was completely unmemorable. I think I may have given him a blowjob before we spooned and he put Savage Garden on to sing along to before falling asleep. The next morning he got up and went to work while I stayed in bed and slept for most of the day. I eventually grew the balls to venture downstairs because I was starving and despite being in my pyjamas ended up sitting in the garden with two of his housemates. Mr Disappointment said he'd hated one of them but I thought he seemed alright as he offered me his cigarettes and beer, and we spoke about music as he actually had a clue about what was going on in the scene. It was this chat that made him say "you're way cooler than him" in reference to Mr Disappointment, and I think he may have been right.

When he returned from work, I was showered and dressed nicely for him and we chilled for about five minutes before ordering the Indian I said I'd pay for. Another £50 gone. After we ordered, his mum called and he went outside to talk to her for ages leaving me with one of his housemates again. The food arrived, he came back in, and something about him seemed odd. It probably wasn't his mum at all, and the conversation as we ate was limited. His housemate and his girlfriend joined us again that evening and all was going well with drinking games until the girlfriend told Mr Disappointment that she'd overheard the housemate he hated calling him a lazy cunt. He got way too pissed off about this for any normal person and I told him to forget about it but instead he spent the rest of the night snapping at everybody with steam pouring from his ears.

By the time we went to bed I was quite drunk and he was still in a terrible mood. The sex was disastrous again, he tried to make me come but it wasn't happening and he had trouble keeping it up for the second night running. He still managed to finish fairly quickly before the usual post-sex routine of an immediate shower took place. On the Sunday morning I woke up ridiculously horny and tried every technique to get him to have sex with me. Despite him not starting work until 10, there was nothing happening and he wasn't going to do it no matter how much I begged. He told me he wouldn't be able to text me as he'd run out of data allowance on his pay as you go plan so I didn't hear from him all day.

He came back from work and got his phone out as he was getting changed. There was a text he quickly deleted and he had the same strange look on his face as he had the night before when he'd taken the phone call. The number wasn't saved in his phone, was on text as he had no data for WhatsApp and had a kiss at the end. I'm quite sure it could only have been Zoe POF from Friday night, and he'd been texting her all day whilst at work but I kept my mouth shut for the peace as I knew he'd only have a go about me being mental again. Plus the text had been deleted so there was no proof. He insisted on putting a film on and trying to make me suck him off despite me being starving for actual food. I eventually got my way and we made food from the supplies I'd bought on Friday, and although he apparently wasn't hungry he still ate a massive portion as we again sat in silence. During this time, he somehow managed to convince me to stay another night and to go straight to work the following day which I agreed to even though it meant me getting up at an ungodly hour the next day.

As we watched the film he kept leaning back over the bed to check his phone every few minutes but it was nice to spend some time just the two of us for a change, rather than constantly with his housemates. The sex that night made up for the shit I'd endured the past two evenings, with him finally making me come again and I let him check another thing off his list by coming on my tits. This was after I fell off the bed naked and ended up wedged between his bed and the chest of drawers though (there really wasn't much space in his room at all), which I found hilarious but he seemed less than impressed by and put no effort into pulling me out. After the showers, he decided that he usually slept on his right and wanted to go that way which meant no spooning of any sort. When I got up to leave in the morning he didn't flinch and I snuck out like it had been some kind of weird one night stand.

I called him to wake him up while I was waiting for the train, stupid fucking guilty conscience, and hardly heard from him again all day due to his apparent lack of money on his phone. That week the conversations became fewer and less interesting, with neither of us really having anything to talk about with each other and his sudden mood change. The nice morning messages had completely stopped by this point, he was no longer filthy or flirty, and the soppiness was history but I clung on in there in the hope he'd go back to who he was when we first started talking.

At some point during the early days of that week, he'd asked me if I'd go down again the following weekend as he finally had Sunday off. I hadn't spent a weekend in my bed for a month by this point and really wasn't keen to travel again so asked if he'd come to mine instead if I paid for his train fare. He'd already met my mum so introducing him to my brother wouldn't have been a big deal, and it meant I wouldn't have to spend as much money on food because there was stuff at home for us to eat. I fretted about asking this for a day when he actually agreed quite willingly which I was surprised about.

On the Wednesday and Thursday came the next issue. On Wednesday he disappeared again, so I did my usual routine of checking his POF. He'd been online that day. Again. Despite him saying that exact day that he hadn't signed in for ages. AGAIN. On the Thursday morning I woke him up as normal, then decided to bring it up because I was massively bothered and sent him a text which colleagues helped me construct. I put no anger in it, just laid out my feelings and was honest about the fact I'd seen him on there. His reply was "I'll speak to you later xx" That was it. Of course, he probably wanted the day to think of an excuse and to let me wallow and think I was in the wrong.

When we spoke that evening, he started off with the pleasantries before launching into a rant about my text that morning. Texting rather than talking had annoyed him, he didn't feel the need to delete POF yet, and he still got notifications and occasionally went on out of curiosity but wasn't talking to anyone. He said he didn't care if I was talking to anyone else because he didn't get jealous but would be annoyed if I was meeting up with people. I'm not sure talking to other people was a matter of jealousy, more of a matter of respect as

I'm not sure it would have been appropriate to have still been lurking online. The way he spoke when we had an issue was so aggressive I couldn't argue back. It always ended up with him having a go at me, me somehow being brought round to his way of thinking and only realising a few hours later how ridiculous he was. After our conversation I filled my friends in, saying I was alright with the whole situation but that was due to having the wool pulled over my eyes again.

    Later on he asked if I still wanted him to come down that weekend. We planned for him to come straight to mine on the Saturday when he finished work and to go home the following day. I transferred the train ticket money and he said "you'll never guess what happened, when I withdrew that £20 for the train it was a fake note". Well that never happens. He went on for a bit before I interjected with "I haven't got any more money to give you" to which he replied "no no I know, I'll figure it out" and nothing about it was mentioned again.

    Saturday rolled around and I was in a great mood. Despite spending my last bit of money on food again for us, I was waking up with no rush to do anything for the first time in ages, went to the gym and went and saw my nan telling her all about Mr Disappointment before heading home to start getting ready for his arrival. Unfortunately, this good mood was soon ruined by him. When he left work he called me and to say he was snappy would be an understatement. He was huffy and stroppy, and insisted on me staying on the phone to hear all of this throughout the duration of his journey bringing me down with him.

When he pulled into the station he asked which way to go and apparently didn't understand the instruction of "right, then left". He shouted at me a lot, saying my sense of direction is shit (it isn't) and in the end I snapped back saying he should have just fucking stayed at home. He asked if I'd got any alcohol in which I hadn't as I couldn't afford it so he asked me to direct him to the nearest shop because he needed a bottle of vodka. Somehow he could afford that even though he couldn't afford to pay for the train. When he got to the bus stop I told him I was going for a while to get ready, mainly because I was fucking furious and needed to calm down before he arrived at my house. His phone was still apparently out of action but he'd managed to be on WhatsApp during the bus ride too which annoyed me further, and he called me again soon after to ask where to get off. My sense of direction wasn't so shit that time and he knocked on my door shortly after.

He gave me a hug when he arrived which I was less than enthusiastic about and as usual he went straight to the kitchen for me to feed him. He could tell I was annoyed and was trying really hard to be nice but no part of me wanted him near me or in my home. We spent the evening on separate sofas and I rejected his ask for a kiss after he pissed me off some more by refusing to shut the door when he came in, instead just sitting down and laughing. As the night drew to a close I really did not want to have sex with him. He put Match of the Day on and I tried to go to sleep so I'd have an excuse when bedtime came. My mum came in shortly after and ended up sitting with us because he was too engrossed in the football to move, and we didn't go to bed until about 1am.

	Sex was initiated by him and I gave it a half-hearted shot. It didn't last very long but as I was getting into the swing of it he pulled out without warning and came all over my tits again. Thanks for that. I got up and showered, and when I got back into the bedroom he was asleep with his back towards my side. If murder were legal, I would have seriously considered smothering him in his sleep at this point. We slept back to back and I woke up at 7am still reeling from all of the events from the previous night while he stayed in bed until midday. I texted my friend for a massive rant on how much of a cock he'd been with her agreeing that it all seemed a bit much, and tried to act normal as I didn't want my mum knowing how he'd behaved while he was still in the house.

He text me when he was awake and I went into the bedroom with my laptop as I was halfway through applying for a job. I got into bed with it and he got sulky again because I wasn't paying him any attention. He got up and got dressed, almost crying over a spot he had on his face before pulling out a bottle of foundation to cover it up with. What the fuck is that. Do all men wear make-up secretly? I'm not sure that they do. We got up so I could make the pre-planned bacon sandwiches and he sat in with my mum as he moaned about how much I'd fucked up the pizzas the night before. I just hadn't cremated them and it would seem that's how he liked it. We ended up eating at different times and I didn't even care.

My mum went out for a while and rather than making full use of an empty house, we sat and watched TV all fucking day. I don't even sit and watch TV on my own so I was bored shitless and was still being a bitch to him because I hated him and wanted him gone. Eventually he asked why I was being such a hater and I tried to make an effort to be a bit nicer, inviting him onto the sofa with me for a cuddle. When I went for a shower he said he'd blow dry my hair again like he had the first time he stayed so I let him know when I was out to which he replied "yeah in a minute". In a minute wasn't quite in a minute as he asked me to put more food in for him before he got in the shower. We ended up clearing out most of the freezer, then he insisted on me sitting in the bathroom to keep him company while he showered. Of course he asked a few times if I would suck him off to which I declined as I'd had no sex all day while the family was out so didn't think he deserved a blow job.

    We ate and spent the evening in the living room again after he decided he'd be staying another night. I didn't invite him or offer it but apparently he didn't want to go home so said he'd go straight to work the next morning. The sex that night was fairly good and he made me watch The Only Way is Essex before asking me to spoon him to sleep. Another man asking me to spoon them, for god sake. The next morning he got up early and left, and I walked him to the door to kiss him goodbye. Although he'd pissed me off all weekend something inside me didn't feel ready to let him go yet so I thought maybe we'd work it out. Little did I know that would be the last time I ever saw him.

The following week I decided to tell him in a subtle manner all the things about him that were annoying me. I told him he never said nice things or sent a nice message which was apparently because he was tired from working six days a week. I said I wasn't paying for anything anymore as I was fed up with being his meal ticket, and I said I didn't feel like he made much of an effort anymore, to which he replied "I spend every evening on the phone to you, that's loads of effort". Talking to someone you're trying to woo on the phone is not effort, especially when it's them calling you at your request all the time because you're too poor to use your phone properly. During this conversation he told me "I'm 26 and I'm not dicking about, I thought I'd be a dad now which is why I'm taking it slow to make sure the next person I'm with is the one forever". I don't even fucking want kids. We'd had this talk at the beginning but he insisted I would once I found the right person. Also, this was not taking it slow. This was talking all the time, spending nights together when we saw each other, me being willing to pay for him but him not wanting to call me his girlfriend so it was almost acceptable for him to talk to other girls.

We carried on for the next week and the morning messages and effort restarted for a few days before he couldn't be arsed again. I had a week off work approaching and he asked what I had planned. I reminded him he'd said he'd come to the Natural History Museum with me to which he replied "we'll talk about that another time". That's a no then.

On the following Friday night, I ended up getting hammered and spoke to two of my friends about the situation who tried to convince me to check his POF again. I said no to which they replied "that's because you know deep down it was today". I cried a lot that night about how shit it had all turned with Mr Disappointment and went home fairly early. I'd tried to call him four times which he'd ignored and before he could contact me I got in and checked when he'd last been online on POF as the idea was stuck in my drunken head. It had been that day. Suddenly it didn't seem like much of a coincidence anymore and I text him telling him I was sick of him making me feel like an option and how I was done. He replied having a go at me before changing his Facebook status to "Mugged off again… Nice one [his name] #stayingsingle". HOW HAVE I MUGGED YOU OFF IN THIS SITUATION?! I went to bed without replying to his text and woke up at 6am to make sense of what had just happened.

He'd deleted me off Facebook and hadn't text me again. I was so hurt and angry, I text him saying I couldn't believe his actions and how he hadn't bothered to talk it out properly with me when I was sober. I ended up calling him to talk about it but the same usual pattern followed. He took his aggressive tone telling me he'd pressed POF accidentally and how he didn't see why this was an issue again when we'd only spoken about it the week before. If he hadn't constantly insisted of his own accord that he wasn't using it, it wouldn't have been an issue. He'd broken his own fucking stupid honesty policy.

I spent the afternoon talking it all over and realising how much of a cock and a loser he was. I didn't need him in my life so I text him when I got home saying it was over. He replied saying he respected my decision but it was a shame as he'd deleted POF after our chat that morning. Obviously I checked and, surprise surprise, his account was still active. I told him this and he sent me a screenshot of his phone screen. He'd just deleted the app. For some stupid reason I then convinced myself that he thought deleting the app meant deleting his profile and we ended up going back to chatting and almost back to normal. I still wasn't ready to let him go, I don't know why but I just couldn't and after spending the day in tears I was emotionally drained.

The next week we got on ridiculously well and things seemed to be looking up. I think this may have been because he was miserable for reasons he wouldn't tell me, and when he was miserable he didn't have the energy to go out of his way to be a cock and was quieter, nicer, and needier than he was when he was happy. Yes I know. Good relationships are not built on the foundations of one person being miserable and lacking energy to horrible.

I had an essay due that week and was stressed but was managing it as I'd got an extension to give myself an extra week. I'd planned to crack on every evening but on Wednesday Mr Disappointment text me to say he'd had a call about a job but his lack of properly functioning laptop meant he was unable to sort his CV out so I'd have to do it for him. After trying to direct him on how to use the shit little netbook he had, he emailed the text of his CV to me for me to grammatically correct and format for him. It took me all evening which I did while he casually watched the football and rather than any kind of thank you he nit-picked stupid little things for me to change as I started getting snappy with him. There was one evening wasted.

The next day I woke him up as per usual and we had a few texts in the morning before he said "I'm really miserable again today". I asked what was going on and he replied with "I'll talk to you later, I don't want to hide anything from you". Way to make a girl on edge all day. We didn't speak much after that as I wasn't sure what I was meant to say, and when I called him that evening and asked him to tell me what was going on he said "don't worry about it, it doesn't matter". After all that?! As if I'm backing off that easily. I pushed until he told me and he finally came out with "I've got myself into a mess with payday loans, it's really bad. I've got no money or anything, moved into this single room because I couldn't afford my last place, and that's why I don't eat unless I'm with you". I had a feeling it was money related and had prepared myself all day for him to tell me he had a problem with gambling as that's what my gut told me. He said that no one knew, the interest on it was crippling him, the company wouldn't freeze it, and no debt charities would help him as it was less than £2000. I spent that evening helping him find a solution, and eventually came up with one that worked. Rather than saying he'd do it, after all my hours of effort he replied with "Nah I just need someone to lend me £1000 to pay it off". Well the chances of that happening are quite unlikely seeing as it seems like the only friends you have are girls you've met online, but good luck.

It all started when he'd moved away from his hometown three years previously but he promised it would be sorted in a few months' time, and that this was why he hadn't asked me to do anything recently after I said I wouldn't be paying anymore. He then gave some spiel about how he was scared to tell me in case I thought he was a loser and got rid of him. He then asked what my credit card limit was and asked if he could borrow a grand. That would be a no. After this chat things didn't feel the same at all. I'd just spent another evening on him when I should have been doing my essay and when Friday came around the next day again I decided that a stiff drink was needed and went for a couple after work. On my way home I tried to call him a few times and his phone was engaged for ages. I texted telling him to let me know when he was off the phone and got no reply, and when I called again a couple of hours later he pretended his phone hadn't been working and said he'd been asleep. I knew his asleep voice and that was not it.

Over the weekend we barely spoke and when we did it sounded like he couldn't be arsed. He mentioned a few times that if he got an interview for this job he'd need a haircut otherwise he wouldn't feel confident but he couldn't afford it, and it got to the point where I was certain he was hinting for me to pay for it. I, of course, did not offer to do that. He also told me he couldn't talk on Saturday night because he was drinking with his housemate and his girlfriend, and must have forgotten that I had been involved in a few of these nights and knew they weren't so eventful that he couldn't take a quick phone call.

When we spoke on the Monday he was much more of the same, and when I tried to call before bed his phone was again engaged. The Tuesday contact was limited. He sent a blunt reply to my text and two ridiculous Snapchats to all of his contacts including me instead. This pissed me off massively because I knew everyone on his Snapchat was girls and he seemed to be in a great mood in those pictures in comparison to the miserable bastard he was in his text. When I spoke to him in the evening he said he was going to make some calls to see who would lend him this sought for £1000. He even started looking through his phone book and asked if it was unreasonable to ask his first ex-girlfriend for it as she'd recently got back in touch to tell him her dad was pretty much on his death bed. Yes, I'd say it's definitely unreasonable to ask her. I told him to let me know when he was free to chat, which he didn't, so went to bed with my 'enough is enough' head on. It had to end, and pronto as I had been mugged off one too many times by this gold digging man over the past nine weeks. I was officially done.

    I woke up late the next morning, and rather than rushing whilst repeatedly pressing redial on my phone to wake him up I thought he could fuck off and wake himself up for a change. This didn't go down well, despite him not sending any nice messages to wake up to for weeks and he text me with "Where's my morning call?". I told him I was running late and he threw a tantrum over me apparently being very aggressive when I said "It feels like you're pieing me off" after questioning his distance. Not sure how that phrase could ever be aggressive but ok pal, whatever helps you to sleep easy at night. We left it at an agreement to speak later that evening as I psyched myself up all day to finally put an end to it.

    The phone call followed the exact same pattern as all previous ones had. His tone was harsh and violent, and I couldn't say anything because I was upset. He came out with a whole bunch of clangers including "you've made no effort to come down for an evening for dinner and drinks", yeah because you recently told me I'd have to foot the bill despite you being a cunt, "you're tarring me with the same brush you have for your exes", nope, you're just a horrible person, "why didn't you just wait until you came down Saturday to see how things were then?", so I could stock your cupboards for you first? No thanks. And the best one "you'll struggle to find anyone else who will put up with you and your issues". OHHH so I'm just meant to settle for you am I?! Fuck off. That one put the nail in the coffin. I was on the verge of tears and said "can I call you later?" before hanging up and finally finishing my essay the night before it was due. I didn't call him later and had no intention of ever speaking to that tosser again.

    The funny thing is, throughout all the time we were talking he would regularly say that he never chases people. That night he sent me some bullshit text like "I guess you don't want to talk again then". Well, no. Then the next day he sent me one in the evening saying "This is exactly what I meant when I said you seemed like you didn't care. You've proved it". Good, I'm glad I've proved it. You caused me feeling like this, you piss off and deal with it in your shit little single bedroom in a town with no friends, and with absolutely no fucking money to entertain yourself. I contemplated replying to both of these messages before realising it wasn't worth the hassle and he didn't deserve any kind of nice explanation from me after the way he'd behaved during this time. The next day, two days after we last spoke, I received the last texts from him. "I'm not sure when you turned into this person with such a lack of respect and courtesy" and then, to follow on his statement about respect, he text again saying "Fine, be an ignorant cunt". I was fucking furious. I don't mind the word cunt, in fact I welcome it, but when it's said by a man to a woman in a genuinely aggressive tone I have not got time for that. I cried at work, I told my brother and he was almost ready to drive to Mr Disappointment's work to knock seven shades of shit out of him, and I then decided it was time to block him. I blocked him on WhatsApp, Snapchat, Plenty of Fish when I saw he returned to it on the Sunday and Facebook (even though I'd resent a friend request earlier in the week to see how he responded and he'd ignored it).

    That was it. I was done, free from his fucking misery forever. The first few days were horrendous. Despite him being such a bastard I missed having someone constantly on the end of the phone so much and I was so disappointed that the man I thought I'd met at the beginning didn't turn out to be anything like how he actually was. That's how the name was born and that is what he is. A complete disappointment in every way, shape and form.

An Open Letter to Mr Disappointment

As I could never say what I wanted to Mr Disappointment, after the events happened and when it was all fresh I thought the best way to get it out would be to put it in the book, naturally. The open letter below came before the chapters and I debated removing it afterwards but this was my closure. Here's to hoping he reads it one day and thinks up some entertaining excuses to pass the blame all back onto me. Again.

Dear Mr Disappointment,

I hope that one day this reaches you and I'm finally able to say my piece without you shouting at me or making up shit excuses to make me seem unreasonable. No doubt you're still not taking any of the blame for anything so I expect if you do read this, you're already sat there cussing and calling me all kinds of names. Forever the victim, aren't you?

However, now that you've been blocked from all forms of communication and I can see and think straight without you, the emotional vampire, coming in and being a cock I can look back on the past nine weeks and really see what a horrible human being you are.

Firstly may I just say that for someone who 'doesn't chase people' you really have gone above and beyond this week. Although I realise now that you never said that for saying its sake, you said it as a threat for in case I ever did have a problem and walked away from you. You never expected me to actually do it did you? Really thought you'd hooked me in. I can also see that this was just another way of you trying to keep all control over the situation. My complete lack of reply has probably been winding you up no end because you know that all the control is in my hands. Four texts in less than 48 hours you sent before I blocked you from WhatsApp, and I really hope you tried to send more as the frustration when you realised you'd been cut-off from there too would have been hilarious.

You spoke all about how communication is important but here's the thing. Every time I had a problem I told you. You had an easy solution every time and it could have been talked out but instead you adopted that fucking aggressive tone and went at me, making me seem unreasonable and temporarily brainwashing me with your shit excuses. Every problem I had could have easily been resolved if you weren't so selfish and stubborn.

When I told you I'd seen you'd been online on Plenty of Fish and was upset about it, you were the one with the shit communication. Any girl who'd invested that much time and effort in someone after a month of seeing each other in real life would be upset by that and looking back, you shouting "I'm single I can do what I want" probably wasn't the best way to handle it. I didn't even ask you to delete it, I said I'd be happier if they were deleted yet you blamed me for trying to trap you and for giving you orders.

The same thing happened again at six weeks after you'd spent a weekend with me and my family but this time you knew I meant it when I tried to end it which is why you fed me "I don't see myself as single but I don't see myself as in a relationship" and why you deleted the app (couldn't even be bothered to delete your full profile).

During the last shout you had you started bringing all this up again when I mentioned nothing about it. You even went back to "I'm single I can do what I want". All I'd said was that you seemed distant this week but you took it as an excuse to have a go at me again. You also said that I'm the one who makes no effort as I hadn't been down for an evening to go for dinner or drinks. You told me the previous week you're in a lot of debt and can't afford to pay for anything for the foreseeable future, so do you really think that after shouting you're single I'll be coming down to foot the bill for your evening out? Don't think so.

Your financial situation and your personality are both two completely separate deal-breakers. The fact that you've been in debt for three years and kept talking about how you just needed someone to lend you money to get rid of it shows you have no intention of sorting your own life out, and I'm quite sure that a part of you thought I might even lend you £1000. No chance. You also blamed the fact that you didn't say nice things or send the occasional thoughtful message anymore on you being tired from working so much, but no one is ever too tired to send a text and thoughtfulness costs nothing. You're just a lazy fucking bastard who expects someone to come along and make you their world without giving anything to them in return.

There's been two things you've said this week that have really shown the kind of person you are, the first one being during your rant on Wednesday when you said "I've been very tolerant with you, you'll struggle to find anyone else who will put up with you." Well you know what, even if that were true I'd still rather be single than settle for you. Remember the article I sent you when we first started talking about how people shouldn't want to be tolerated by a partner but instead should want to be the best person they can be for them? You're not even nearly the best person you could be. I made far too much effort with you, gave you too much support when you had problems and you gave me absolutely nothing in return. Take a look at your own life and I think you'll see that if anyone will struggle to find someone else it'll be you. Even if you do find a poor woman who will believe your convincing that she can't do any better she will definitely just be 'putting up with you' rather than enjoying being with you.

The second thing you've said was the last text you sent me before I blocked you completely out of my life. "Fine be an ignorant cunt." I have no problem with the word cunt at all, but when it's meant in a genuinely aggressive manner from someone who is still trying to pass the blame, and from a man to a woman it shows how vile you are. Especially as the text you sent before that spoke all about 'respect and courtesy'. Is it respectful to call a woman a cunt? A woman who fed you for three weekends in a row because you're skint, put up with your lack of effort but still called you every morning to wake you up, and spent two evenings the week before trying to sort your life out when those evenings needed to be spent doing an assignment that the deadline was looming for? Let's not forget how I was stressed about this and yet rather than offering any kind words a few days later you simply said "fucking hell you're miserable".

I can see now why you were so angry every time I spoke to other people about us. It's not because you're a private person as you say, it's because you know deep down that the way you treated me was disgusting. You were more than happy for me to tell people about you in the beginning while you were pretending to be someone perfect, but as that mask slipped and you couldn't be bothered to keep up the pretence anymore you'd hit the roof if I told you I'd spoken about things with friends. My friends are always honest with me because they know I respect them for that, and every person I've told about you during the last month has been praying for me to bin you. Now I have, everyone apart from you is happy and that is what I call karma.

Yours sincerely,

Your alarm clock, your crutch of support, your meal ticket, and the best thing that could have ever happened to you had you not been such a massive knob.

The Return and Speedy Exit of Mr Disappointment

I had made it through a whole weekend of no contact with Mr Disappointment and was halfway through the next week. Admittedly I was still heartbroken and angry, but I was coping. The root cause of my anger had been the way it was all left. I'm not the kind of person who can easily walk away from an argument letting the other person think they're right when they're not, and there were so many things I should have said to him instead of taking the blame for everything to make him just walk away and leave me alone. Of course, with this one that was the only way I could have played it. Had I said my piece he would have turned it all back on me and the circle would have been continuing forever, for the rest of my damn life and I wasn't keen for that.

      Exactly a week after I last spoke to him, he managed to contact me again. On Wednesday 16th

April he tried to call me and when his name flashed up on my screen my heart when into my stomach. It wasn't over yet, and he was still doing a bloody good job of chasing me even though he insisted he never did that. I didn't answer and I burst into tears before receiving a long bullshit text message from him apologising for calling me a cunt saying that he thought it might just get a reaction out of me, asking if we could talk, blah blah blah blah blah. I replied back saying it was funny he called me such a thing straight after talking about respect, quoted back some of the things he'd said to me on that last phone call, said I wasn't sure what he ever wanted from me, and that I didn't want to speak to him. He came back simply with "Please call me, you don't need to talk just hear me out". I told him I didn't think it was a good idea because his aggressive tone just upset me, and that I'd think about it for a few hours.

After lying on my bed crying for a few hours and thinking it all through (I know, pathetic), I called him. I shouldn't have, I'm a mug, but I called him. He was clearly making a conscious effort to speak in a rational tone and he said things like "I don't think I realised how strongly you felt about everything until you sent that text earlier", you mean how much of a dick you were, and "I want you in my life still". He even said "if we just be friends now there's a chance something might happen in the future". Why would I want to be with you in the future? Why oh fucking why would I want to be your friend and hang about in the hope you might decide you want to be with me? Oh yeah, I wouldn't. I wonder if that's what rubbish he gave to previous POF girls, or the girls filling up his Snapchat friends list.

Of course, when all this was being said I was completely blind sighted again. I don't know what it is about this kid but every time he fed me shit I just lapped it up. Who does that? He's like Houdini or something, the world's greatest fucking illusionist.

Another thing he said which I didn't even think about until a few days later was that on the Friday night when I checked up on him to see if he'd been into his online dating profile it had "massively put him off". Hang on. So why then did you go out of your way to try and get me back by deleting the app? Why did you waste two of my evenings on your problems? And why did you get so angry when I caused the row during our last conversation? Probably because you wanted me to feed you and give you money.

We ended up on the phone for about an hour and were getting on well towards the end, like we had during our good times. The next day I decided that if this friendship were to go ahead there would be ground rules and I texted him to tell him this, and asked him to let me know when he was free to talk. We spoke that evening and the ground rules were recited from a notepad document I'd jotted down on my phone. They were as follows:

• Stop lying.

He told me he'd been on POF the night before to try and message me and saw he was blocked. I knew he'd been on a few days previously. When this was brought up to him he swore on his niece's life he hadn't. So much for being 'family orientated' as his weak profile stated.

• I don't want to hear about girls.

He laughed this one off and made a joke about my jealousy again. For fuck sake.

• I don't want to hear about money issues.

He went quiet when I said this one, as if the ball had finally dropped about me really not giving him any funding, but he agreed to it all the same.

When we hung up, we had a laugh and called each other 'mate' which he forbid me to do at the beginning, before he said "you can send me a message". I did send him a message a couple of hours later, and despite him being online all evening it took him two hours to reply. He asked no questions, made no conversation, and referred to nothing that I had said. I sent another message. The same routine followed. Suddenly it clicked. All this shit about wanting me in his life was just another control game for him. He wanted me back in the palm of his hand as a fish in his pond of women that he ducked into to get what he wanted. Just as I'd started sleeping better again, this night's sleep was completely broken and I was back to waking up in the early hours with my brain cogs whirring. I didn't want to do this. I didn't want him in my life, and I didn't even like him enough as a person to entertain the thought of checking in occasionally to see how he was. Fuck this.

The next day was Good Friday and I'd planned a day trip out of town to see my friend. As we hadn't spoken properly in ages she was completely unaware of the Mr Disappointment story so I told her it in full. It took around four hours and laying the whole thing out there in front of me made me even more angry that I'd let him worm his way back in. I ignored his text that day and the question mark he sent me when I didn't respond, and text him the next morning saying "I'm not ready to be your friend. The thought of you still makes me angry and sad and I need a few weeks away from you. I'm not saying this to be a cunt, I'm saying this for the sake of my own sanity so I hope you respect that." I threw in his reference to him calling me a cunt on purpose and used the last line to ensure he didn't try and get me to talk about it again. He came back with "No worries. Take care." And with that I blocked him from everything else possible to make sure he really wouldn't be coming back. He was blocked on my phone so he couldn't call or text, blocked again on WhatsApp, blocked on both email accounts, and all other barriers had still remained in place so there was no way for him to get through.

    That was the last time I heard from him which is hardly surprising as the only other way he could contact me would be to knock on my door and we all know he can't afford the train fare for that kind of gesture.

    However, there was one incident involving him a month or so later. On one of the weekends I went down to visit I had made an amazing old school playlist on my YouTube account but as my phone was dying I'd logged into my account on his phone so we could plug in to the speakers. During a phone conversation a few days later I asked if he'd logged out, to which he said "yes" in a tone that tried to prompt me to give him my password. It turns out he wasn't logged out at all. Whilst sat at work with YouTube open on my computer I had a weird video pop up on my 'recommended' section that wasn't even mildly related to anything I have ever watched. So I went onto my history. Not only was he still using my old school playlist, clearly knowing that he was indeed still logged in, but my history was full to the rafters with gambling videos and brutal real life fight compilations. What kind of fucking headcase sits and watches hour upon hour of this kind of thing? Mr Disappointment, that's who. I changed my password knowing that it would log me out of every device I'm signed into, including his phone, then remembered the way he'd casually ask me for passwords to things all the time. I feared he may have been making some kind of mental note of them so I then had to go through every account I have to change them all.

      And that was it. The complete and utter end of him. No more returns, no more nasty surprises, but a heart that felt like it had been through a blender and the return of the ice queen in full force. I knew I had a book to write but I didn't want to spend time with any man, couldn't be bothered to talk to any man, and only wanted to have sex with another man in the hope that I would be getting laid sooner than he would. There I was, mid-April not knowing what the fucking hell to do about this gaping hole that some stranger I never really knew had left. The whirlwind of it had left my brain mush and it wasn't until the beginning of June that I finally felt over it.

My apologies readers, but you can't say I didn't warn you. I understand if you need 27 alcoholic beverages after all of that but you can be sure that part is over now. Good news! I'm funny again, startiiiiing… NOW.

The Cancelled Dates

In between the final row and the return of Mr Disappointment I attempted to get back in the game for the book's sake and ended up in conversation with two men on Plenty of Fish. First was Mr Conversation, an Irish man in his late 20s who I ended up in an essay-off with due to the absolute beasts of messages that were exchanged between us about nothing in particular. The second, Mr Heartbroken; a 21 year old estate agent who could apparently tell I was everything he could ever need from just a few texts (probably a wrong assumption, sorry pal).

I didn't have any particular feelings for either of these men due to the shit that went down with that last bellend so effort was quite minimal on my part. There were no phone calls, no talk of social media or Snapchat exchanges on either end, and no personal information imparted. Both were converted onto the text quite quickly with dates arranged early on. It all felt a bit much as they were both incredibly keen and all of my chirpsing was carried out begrudgingly as opposed to genuinely looking for a person to have in my life.

The first planned date with Mr Conversation was a provisional booking as I forewarned him I could be hungover. When the day rolled round, I was indeed a bit hungover but mainly just didn't want to go as it was the day after I'd sent the final text to Mr Disappointment and cut him off. As the conversation between us continued over the next couple of weeks he seemed to grow more and more keen whereas I grew more and more not bothered. He said something about me and my humour being 'perfect for him', and on one night out he text me saying "It's so weird I'm in a bar full of women and I'd rather stand here texting a girl I've never met". Honestly mate you really don't have to do that. A bit later on I got "I like you" and a few drunk dials which fortunately I missed due to being busy sleeping. I was in the frame of mind where everything a man said to me would instantly be responded to with "BULLSHIT" in my head.

Mr Heartbroken ran alongside Mr Conversation and never had very much to say for himself apart from attempts at arranging a date. I was reluctant because he was only just out of puberty but a date was arranged all the same. That same date was cancelled the day it was meant to happen. I didn't hear from him for a long time after this but he occasionally popped up to tell me I'd broken his heart or other such bollocks.

I don't know where my head was at but it certainly wasn't in the game. I am a wallower of epic proportions and I take my hat off to all women who get straight back on the saddle after one terrible encounter because I certainly can't do it. My intolerance for other human beings had hit a peak. All I wanted to do was go home and chill with my dog because he doesn't ask me to tell him about myself, I've known him long enough to feel comfortable snuggling up on the sofa with him, and I don't even need to put on make-up or a bra to be in his company. He also doesn't judge me for being a smoker, doesn't check out my gunt to see if it's bigger in real life, and really doesn't mind that I don't like or want children. Who needs men when you've got pets?

Another date was arranged with Mr Conversation and during the build-up I just didn't want to go. I was trying to psych myself up to just get on with it but it wasn't happening. Then he said something that put the nail in the coffin. He said the words which make my skin crawl, which Mr Disappointment had said, as had Mr Out of Proportion, as had the two terrible experiences I had in my early twenties. He said "I'm a nice guy".

What's wrong with that, you may wonder. Nice guys do not say "I'm a nice guy", nice guys prove they're nice guys. They know its actions over words, and that saying that is as empty as me saying "I look just like Tina Turner". Of course I don't look like Tina Turner, I'm white for a start. But you see my point. Anyone can say they're a nice guy, and people who have said it to me before have been anything but. Sorry Mr Conversation but I don't want any more of you guys that say they're nice near me. This is not happening.

    During this time I was still in polite-mode, as I thought that's how you should act with so rather than actually calling bullshit and starting a row with someone I'd never met, when the day came round I dropped a hint that I didn't feel very well. I actually didn't feel great but most of that was probably the wear and tear on my soul at the thought of going on a date with a "nice guy". He text back saying he hoped I felt better soon before carrying on the conversation through the day. As afternoon approached he asked how I was feeling to which I responded "Still not great". Mr Conversation came back with "Oh no, I hope you feel better soon… So is 8 alright for tonight? I thought we could go to these places…" Woah, what? I've just told you I don't feel very well, what part of that didn't you get?

Of course I don't want to go on a bloody bar crawl with you and 8pm is not alright, neither is any other time soon or ever. I didn't say that either, instead I apologised and said I needed to reschedule then slagged him off to my friends. He replied with something wet and I never heard from him again. A few weeks later he changed his WhatsApp profile picture and I was suddenly very glad I didn't meet him. Not attractive. I'm not even sure I would have even been able to drunkenly sleep with that for the sake of getting over one by getting under another, and if I had I would have regretted it more than the Ed Miliband lookalike.

The Birth of 15 Matches, 1 Question and the Sudden Influx of Toyboys

For those of you unfamiliar with the dating app Tinder, allow me to explain. People pop up on your phone screen with their name, age, and how far away from you they are. It tells you if you have any mutual friends or interests as its run through Facebook, and you either swipe left for no or right for yes. If you both say yes you get what's called a 'match' and it's only when you match with someone that you can message each other. Simples.

It's through this app that my game began. 15 Matches, 1 Question. The concept is easy, you keep swiping until you get 15 matches then you blanket message those poor unsuspecting bastards with the same copy and pasted message. Some men will use their initiative and message you before you get the chance to include them in the next round, so if that happens just keep swiping until you have 15 fresh and untouched ones. Not untouched as in they're still virgins, untouched as in you're yet to speak to them on Tinder. I'm not a complete pervert.

My first round of this game came towards the end of mine and Mr Conversation's fling. I got my 15 and I sent them the question "Have you got any raisins?" the answer of course being "How about a date?" A girl using a chat up line, how 21st century of me. The response was quite high but we didn't hit 15 out of 15, and some conversations dried up fairly quickly after the punchline had been given. It would seem there's a lot of people who just like the ego boost of a match and don't want to talk. Fucking timewasters.

From this round I got two younger men on the regular contact business, Mr Exaggerator who was 22 and Mr Nice but Dim who had just turned 23. Deciding which one was my favourite was a constant debate that changed every day and I had games going with both of them which was a lot more fun than the generic "Hi, how are you?". With Mr Exaggerator, we had a 'weird photo' competition where we'd take it in turns to take pictures of weird things and exchange them over WhatsApp. The winner was to be decided by us and the loser had to buy the drinks despite no date being set for a couple of weeks. Photos included defaced pictures of people in newspapers, a fight scene using the props on my desk at work, and a selfie with my childhood teddy from me, and a Bart Simpson stool, a fat dog ornament, and a selfie with some man Uggs from him. The winner however, was never decided as naturally we both thought our own photos were the best.

With Mr Nice but Dim, the game was a bit different. From the outset of our messages, we added a question onto the end which started in a fairly safe manner and covered the general subjects such as food, film, and what we did for fun. After a few days of this the questions started becoming more risky and turned sexual. These questions were never surrounded by any filthy or flirty talk though, it was all more FYI and no matter how many times I tried to be suggestive Mr Nice but Dim didn't bite and seemed to just be storing the information rather than commenting on any of it.

Mr Exaggerator was moved onto text fairly quickly, whereas Mr Nice but Dim took a bit longer to ask for my number. In the early stages I didn't mind as much as the slow pace was what I needed. Dates were set for both of them with a week in between the two and despite not winning the photo competition Mr Exaggerator claimed he'd be still buying the drinks as, according to him, he was definitely punching with me. A nice but strange comment I thought, as the pictures he'd sent me showed quite a nice looking young man and, if anything, I'd say we were on par.

The date with Mr Exaggerator was cancelled due to him being horrifically hungover, and rescheduled to the day before I'd arranged to meet Mr Nice but Dim. You know what they say about men and buses. I was in the zone for the two days of dates, didn't feel nervous, and felt ready to get back on it. This could have been because I was absolutely knackered and my body didn't have the energy to feel fear, but it was nice to get ready for dates without my stomach going mental like it had done in January.

On the day of meeting Mr Exaggerator I wore a see-through top, a skirt, and heeled boots which I didn't think would be a problem as he'd told me he was 5'10" and I'm only 5'2". He lived a 45 minute journey away and had arranged for a friend to drop him off and pick him up so he could have a few drinks with me, and as I was running late (for a change) he awaited my arrival at the train station. When I got there he was a fair distance away and seemed to look just as he had in a picture he'd sent me the week before. Tall, stubbly, reasonably handsome, and not 22 years of age. As he approached, this was all washed away quite quickly. In my shoes I was no taller than 5'5"... And he was no taller than me. His whole body was so small, like a child, and the stubble didn't seem as manly as it had from 20 metres away. I thought people were meant to get bigger as they came closer, not shrink to half their former size. I felt like an absolute beast next to him. Despite losing one of the four stones my frame shouldn't be carrying, I was still twice the width of him and sex would probably have ended in his death by gunt suffocation.

We went for a couple of drinks and my tiredness and disappointment meant the conversation wasn't flowing as well as it should be on a first date. I didn't mention the fact he'd added five inches onto his height but I'm sure he could tell that I spotted the missing measurements. He filled the chat with anecdotes about lads holidays, mentioned a few times that his jacket cost £450, and then casually went on to ask if I do drugs. This was escalating quickly. I think he also forgot I'd told him I'm low maintenance, as when he told me his job could earn him £50k this year there was no kind of impressed glint from me, more of a cringe as money talk makes me die inside. There is nothing more unattractive to me than people who talk about money. After Mr Disappointment the situation had got worse too. I don't care how much a person earns; I just like it to be proved that a person has their own money and that the sole purpose of dating me isn't to spend mine. Don't tell me how much you're on, don't tell me I have to pay for everything; just pretend you're comfortable whether you are or not, and shut up about it already.

After a couple of drinks in one bar Mr Exaggerator suggested moving on to somewhere else so naturally I took him to the same place I'd taken Mr Disappointment and Mr Lips. We had a few cocktails (I insisted on buying one, fuck you and your £50k salary) before he half mentioned getting a hotel room for the night (ignored, that's a no). When discussing whether to get another, he said his friend had left 45 minutes ago and would shortly be arriving to pick him up. He went to the toilet and I called a taxi to pick me up from where we were, not realising that his friend was due into the station which was now on the other side of town. I forced the offer of asking the taxi to pick me up from there instead but when he said "no it's alright" I responded with "ok cool" rather than changing my arrangements anyway as I probably should have done.

The taxi arrived quite quickly and he walked me to it before giving me another massive cringe. You know when someone looks at your lips like they're about to kiss you? He did that. This evening had not gone well enough to end with a snog and I was not drunk enough to go through with it anyway so rather than reciprocating I panicked, swerved, kissed him on the cheek and gave him the most awkward hug ever while he stood there limp and rejected. Horrendous. I got into the taxi and tried not to freak out about how incredibly uncomfortable the parting situation had been whilst simultaneously ignoring small talk from the driver.

When I got home I courtesy texted him to see if he'd managed to find his friend. It was midnight by this point, an hour and 15 minutes after his friend apparently left, but Mr Exaggerator's reply told me that his friend actually hadn't left at all. I'm an awful person. I saw the text on my phone screen but didn't open it as I feared he'd have expected me to keep him company, or worse, invite him to my house. So instead I left him at the station for god knows how long while he waited for his lift home. I half-heartedly text him the next day to say I'd fallen asleep and luckily he was off on holiday so it was left at "Have a nice time". He'd said "Speak when I'm back" but I didn't contact him and he didn't contact me so that was the end of that.

The following day was the Mr Nice but Dim date and his slowness became even more apparent. We were texting all day, had mentioned the evening once or twice, but no set plans had been made. It wasn't until 6pm when I caved and asked him if we were still meeting and if so, what time he wanted to see me. He replied with "Nah, I thought I'd just stand you up! Of course we're still meeting!" Well pal it's 6pm and you've said nothing about it, don't make me look like the idiot here. We arranged to meet at 9pm so I had three hours to piece my face together to hide last night's hangover. He was much more attractive than what I'd been lumbered with the night before, and his incredible body was quite clear despite being fully clothed. The joys of dating a personal trainer.

Mr Nice but Dim's age was also quite obvious. Maybe not looks-wise but in the way he held himself and how he had no idea of what places to go to. He never did nice bars and was more used to the sticky floors of our local Yates. He was tall, asked a lot of questions to make conversation, and bought the first round in a hot bar we couldn't find a seat in before moving onto the next venue. In there he went and got us another drink while I got a table, and he came back with my standard gin and tonic and two cocktails for him as it was apparently buy one get one free. This then meant I had to go and buy my own second one as he was nursing them for hours but hey, at least we have a man here who is clearly comfortable letting a woman pay for an equal share.

     The conversation flowed quite easily and I couldn't take my eyes off his amazing arms all night. I texted all my friends to let them know how good his body was and sat smugly thinking about how good he would look naked. And on top of me. And inside me. Too far? One thing I did slightly overlook and didn't mention to anyone was that he smelt a lot less than fresh. I put it down to the assumption that a body like that probably required a lot of protein so maybe he had some kind of meat sweats going on. Still, the body outshone the smell so we were good.

     Going to a third place was suggested and I of course took him back to my regular date bar. As we went in, the bouncer looked at me in an odd way and it wasn't until afterwards that I realised he was definitely starting to recognise me coming in and out with different men. At least he didn't give the game away, that was nice of him. It was in this place that

Mr Nice but Dim started getting a bit handsy, not touching me up in a pervy way but just letting me know there was some kind of interest there and showing everyone else in there that he was with me. I was gagging for a good snog and I thought he might make the move as we had been talking constantly for a good few weeks and the evening was going well but no such luck. I bought the drinks in there before we moved downstairs and mainly took the piss out of the weird crowd Friday night had brought in. I finished my drink and he offered another one without getting one for himself; someone's clearly on a budget. When we left we decided it was time to end the night in the most appropriate way. In a dirty food place.

As we sat with our chips he told me the story he hadn't wanted to tell earlier in the night for fear of putting me off. The time he got arrested because he punched a phone box. Steady on folks, we've got a wild one over here. He spoke about how it taught him a lesson and how he had to pay a fine, and I can only imagine he cried his whole way through the court process as I'm not convinced he was actually born with any testicles.

When we said goodbye, I reached out for a hug to try and avoid yet another awkward departing but he stopped next to my face and I wasn't sure if he'd put his back out and got stuck or was testing the water for a kiss. I just went for it to get it over with but it was the most awkward kiss ever. Why is everything in my life always so fucking awkward? I went for tongue and he didn't, then he went for tongue and I didn't, then we ended up having some strange peck-off before I got into the taxi. Funnily enough, the combination of the booze and his arms made me think I might love him a little bit so I text everyone to let them know it had gone exceptionally well. He'd told me to text him when I got home but he text me within about 30 seconds of me leaving him, and I went to bed dreaming of being beasted by the best body I'd ever seen.

This burning love was incredibly short-lived as he made no attempt to schedule the next date for a few weeks. The dirty questions had stopped, he still wasn't being filthy or flirty, and despite our long texts, he said nothing of interest whatsoever. I spent most of the time moaning about how boring he was, and ignored his Facebook friend request when he sent one as I couldn't imagine it going anywhere. But then, there was still that bloody body. The one thing that kept me hanging on was the hope of one day seeing it starkers.

A second date was eventually arranged for three weeks after we first met. It seemed as though he could only do a date on a weekend evening even though he never had many plans during the week. This is inconvenient, I thought. However, when date day rolled around I had to reschedule as I was going away the next day and had a lot to sort out. We then rescheduled to the following week. A month in between dates isn't really ideal, and it was almost like having a first date all over again.

We went to the cinema and for a Nandos which, although a slightly inappropriate date for a 24 year old, was quite nice as I love me some Nandos and didn't have to make conversation during the film. No human contact was made while we were watching which wasn't surprising as he was clearly shit at all of this kind of thing, and I paid for Nandos. Equal amount spent again, this really didn't feel like a date, more like two mates spending some Sunday time together. During food he was chatting away making conversation as he did so well and in my head I couldn't stop thinking "attractive, great body, no arrogance, nice guy, talks a lot, asks questions, shows an interest… NO SPARK. SO BORING." Typical. He had a free house the following week and I'd hinted about 100 times for an invite over for all the sex which somehow he hadn't quite picked up on.

I was a bit nervous about our goodbye time as we were both completely sober and the last snog attempt had been a fail of epic proportions. He kissed me, again it was shit, to which he said "for god's sake!" so he clearly knew it too. I asked if he wanted to try again which he took me up on and we had a pretty good go in the street before passers-by started shouting obscenities at us. This clearly wasn't meant to be.

Again he told me to text him when I got home, and again he text me within 30 seconds of leaving me. I was so confused about all of this; it felt like mates, he didn't compliment me or make any verbal suggestion that he was interested, but then he did that.

We continued to talk through the week and the weekend was mentioned. I told him I had no plans to which he finally said "Well there's a free house over here, you're welcome to come over". Of course, being Mr Nice but Dim he made no proper plans and a few days later said he'd had nothing planned on the Saturday night and was free all of Sunday too. To me, that was a sleepover hint but I was so fed up with his hints and shitness by this point I told him my mum had planned an evening in for us on the Saturday as we hadn't spent time together in ages. This was indeed true, but if he'd asked me round properly a few days previously, my Saturday night would have panned out a lot differently.

He'd spoken about how he could walk around naked while he had a free house and on Wednesday he decided it was naked time. We joked about it, then he sent me a Snapchat that evening. I assumed it would be of something boring like his dinner but what I saw when I opened it was actually his naked body with an enlarged angel emoticon covering his penis. What the fuck just happened? I told him I hadn't managed to screenshot it so he sent another one that evening with a banana covering his bits which I still have safely stored on my phone. This burst was short-lived and he unfortunately went back to being dull as fuck the following day.

When Saturday came round he asked if I wanted to go to his on the Sunday for a bit. I said yes and told him I'd arrange it with him the next day. FUCKING FINALLY. However, when I woke up the next day no part of me wanted to go. His lack of filth, flirt and compliments meant I wasn't sure if he actually fancied me and I couldn't bear the thought of being naked next to a body like that when I didn't know if he found me attractive. I'd have felt terrible about myself, wouldn't have enjoyed the sex at all, and risking the situation going that way wasn't worth two bus journeys. I needed sex but my ego was still bruised, and self-preservation is key. I gave him a shit excuse to which he replied normally with a hint of annoyance. Couldn't summon up the balls to tell me he was pissed off, shock. I didn't reply and for the first time in the six weeks we'd been talking he didn't double text me. Game over. I'd been seeing Mr Disappointment for the same amount of time that me and Mr Nice but Dim had been talking. What a fucking contrast.

The Sexual Reawakening and the End of Polite-Mode

After the bore of Mr Nice but Dim, I was really worried that I'd lost my sex drive completely. I hadn't masturbated in ages and I'd have chosen a box of chocolates or ten over a sweaty session between the sheets. He'd sucked the horn out of me with his dullness and I felt like a born again virgin.

Three men snapped me out of it; just a mere few days after Mr Nice but Dim was put to bed (not literally). Mr Former Paedo, named so because I Googled him and found a before and after gym picture and (obviously) he looked like a paedo in the old picture, had been popping in and out of my life for a few weeks. He was the only conversion from the second round of 15 Matches, 1 Question when I asked 15 men "Fancy going dogging?" but no real chat of interest had happened before now. It was also during this week that my third round of the game commenced, with "What's the difference between jam and marmalade?" Obviously the answer is "You can't marmalade your cock into a girl's mouth". Drastic measures had been taken to end my dry spell, and round three resulted in two conversions by Mr Monster Cock and Mr Meh.

The conversation with Mr Former Paedo ramped up with him telling me I'm beautiful, saying he'd shown his friend a picture of me who had said "I'd never get a girl like that". It moved onto things like "The things I'd do to you" and, of course, he went on about how good he was in bed. He tried to convince me to get a train to his house which I was unsure about due to the fear of being murdered and buried under his patio. His response? "Well I am a gentleman… Obviously I'd give you my address to give to someone". I think it would still be too late for that if you did murder me, mate. I continued talking to him all the same, and sent him a recycled picture of my tits in a bra at some point during the week which he apparently wanked himself off over and "came an inhuman amount". My caged animal had been let out and I was massively playing up to it.

Mine and Mr Monster Cock's affair was short lived, and only lasted two days on WhatsApp before he didn't contact me and I didn't contact him, despite wanting to. He was a very handsome man and was a complete filth-bag. Perfect. My dirty talk hit an all-time high, and at one point during one evening he said "I'm going to hold you down by the throat and come in your face, okay?" I didn't even run for the hills, instead I sent him a naked picture where no bits were exposed (which was also sent to Mr Former Paedo) and then asked if I could watch him come via a video on Snapchat. Apparently this request was too far as he hadn't done that before, and was probably the main reason why we didn't talk again. As if my request was too far… that's rich, come on pal. Regardless, he'd helped to awaken a sexual monster within me and I finally felt human and ready to get it in again sometime soon.

Mr Meh and I barely spoke. We had one evening where he asked me filthy questions and I responded, then he messaged me three days later with "I love you". I didn't hear from him again until a few days later when he popped up saying "Ok maybe I just lust you a lot", and so the end of polite-mode started.

These men all just seemed to want someone to talk dirty to them, send them filthy pictures, and had no real interest in meeting at all. Despite all of Mr Former Paedo's suggestions of me going round his, he'd always disappear for a few days when it seemed like plans were on the cusp of being formed then would miraculously reappear a few days later.

For me, if a man just wants sex that's fine. If the amount of effort put into the acquiring of the sex is "Fancy a shag?" after two or three messages it's a no from me as it's likely they'll put the same amount of effort into the sex and it'll be a shit hands free wank for them. However, more messages, a bit of getting to know each other, and at least taking me out for a few drinks before banging and it's a big fat yes, you're through to Judges' Houses. But these men weren't game for that at all and I'd had enough of time wasters. I'm not getting any real pleasure from knowing a man is wanking himself off at home over me; I'm not that easily pleased for crying out loud, a girl needs to close the deal.

It probably didn't help that I was due on this weekend so I hated everyone and wanted all men to die. The first to feel my wrath was Mr Bald who I'd shared about five messages with on Tinder before moving onto WhatsApp. In the space of one morning he'd managed to send me a picture of the most veiny penis I'd ever seen then told me the full history of him and his ex despite me saying "I won't ask". He started the story with "In a nutshell…" and went on for a lot of words before I replied saying "That's a big nutshell" with a picture of This

Morning's agony aunt Denise Robertson pulling a funny face. I then ignored everything he said afterward which included "So who's on top? ;-)" and "Sorry babe". Take your sorry and fuck off.

This was also the day of Mr Meh's return. To his message of "Ok maybe I just lust you a lot" I replied with "Three days to reply… That is a lot of lust". He then tried to crack out some conversation before starting on about how he was imagining me naked. I asked how he knew what that looked like and he said "Because I can see you now". I asked how many fingers I was holding up, his guess was seven, I replied with "No, two. You can guess which two as well" I never heard from him again either.

I felt like a gladiator taking on all the pathetic men on this day, as another one sent me a message on POF saying "I could waste my breath and mention something related to your profile but then I might not even be your type." I replied with "Well at least you tried… Oh wait." Seriously, were these men taking the fucking mick? Absolutely ridiculous, no wonder everyone in the world is single when all men are so completely clueless about the amount of effort they should really be putting in. Unfortunately, I have heard that there are some dirty women out there who will send pictures of their whole minges and respond kindly to the lack of effort sex requests so clearly they're ruining it for everyone as these men just want the easy option every time. We're all going to die alone, either smugly from the amount of strangers we've slept with in our lifetime or with regret for telling too many people to sod off and spending our lives holed up in the comfort of our own homes away from the perverts and with endless supplies of chocolate. Or is that smugness and regret the other way around? At least if you go for the chocolate option you won't have a loose fanny and full house on STI bingo. But then you will be real fat. Such dilemmas.

I'm sorry readers but after this, for a few weeks, I gave up. They were all getting on my nerves and I think it's already quite clear that I hate people and struggle to tolerate them for any purposes.

It was approaching the end of June by this point and I realised I needed a big plan to make the second half of the year something special. Something worth reading about. So I got my head back in the game and I went, as Kanye and Jay Z would say, HAM. Hard as a Motherfucker.

The Mid-Year Review

I cannot believe how quickly the first half of the year has gone. So much has happened, and I think it's fair to say this book and officially being in the dating game has taught me an awful lot. Like the fact I'm not a good player and I don't like people, and how my talk of being business-only was a crock of shit. But still, let's not wallow on my failures. Onwards and upwards.

However, there's one thing this challenge has taught me. It's taught me what I'm attracted to, and what I'm really not attracted to. I always had a vague idea of this but my experiences of men before this year were fairly limited and usually just when very drunk. If I think of how many men I've spoken to since January, whether it's just been a few messages with ones who aren't book-worthy or ones who I've actually come face-to-face with, I've learnt a lot about myself and my preferences. I couldn't tell you how many men I've been in contact with in total but I'd say it's definitely over 100 which is absolutely ridiculous.

Remember at the beginning of the book when I said I didn't feel like I'd experienced enough men to settle down yet? I don't know whether it's over-exposure to all these men this year, turning 25 a week ago or what, but we have a problem. I've been thinking about it for a couple of weeks and I think I want to be in love. Sorry if you just threw up all over yourself upon reading that. I've always been ok with the thought of following in my mum's and my nan's footsteps and spending my adult years alone but I have wanted to experience proper, all-consuming, mutual love at least once. The want for it has never been particularly urgent but I feel like I'm there. I'm ready for a person to be in my life, to love me as much as I love them, to be soppy and weird with, and to do nice things together. Even if only for a few years before he decides he wants kids, I refuse, we have a big argument and break up which of course is inevitable.

Going about this is going to be a task and a half. I don't want any more Mr Disappointments, I don't want someone who drains me of my energies, but I don't want someone who treats me like an absolute princess either. I want an equal relationship and I fear this might be impossible to find.

Here's my theory about modern dating. I've said before about how people are disposable because if you lose one man technology is sat right there with thousands more of them just a click away. Maybe we've all become too selfish and too greedy, always assuming that if someone we're seeing isn't 100% perfect we can just keep moving onto the next one before finding that soul mate. The thing is, relationships and life don't work like that. Who's to say if we met our Mr Perfect they'd love us back? Everyone is on a constant blinkered quest to find The One when The One probably doesn't exist.

We're so used to being able to find exactly what we want on the internet, whether its researching all the names of the Beckham kids, shopping for a pair of shoes, or looking up rude jokes to use as Tinder openers, so why shouldn't technology be able to give us the mould of this perfect person we're envisaging? Well, because there's no honest database of people to sift through away from bullshit-filled dating profiles so the search is an unsatisfying manual one. Don't get me wrong, I know some people get lucky and aren't this awfully way inclined but I can fully admit to falling into this theory before now. People who don't know what they want expect some crap online chemistry test to churn out the person they need, without thinking about what they want for themselves.

The accessibility to so many people is overwhelming and competition is outrageously high. You make a joke on Tinder which the recipient doesn't quite understand? Unmatched and gone forever. Don't fancy seeing someone again because you've just realised they look like Ed Milliband? Ignored and blocked on all routes of communication. It's a tough game to play, especially when rifling through the people still stuck in this phase, but my want for love and my knowing what I want from a person means I must continue to compete with the girls sending box shots, to deal with the over-inflated egos of average looking men who've received too many 'likes' on their Tinder moments, and to make an awful lot more effort during the getting to know and dating stages.

The Second Half Setup

As June came to an end, I'd pied off all the timewasting bellends and realised I had no one left. I had a week of quiet time and reflection before deciding how to proceed, and then put in an absolute shitload of effort to acquire more men. All men were products of two rounds of my Tinder game 15 Matches, 1 Question, and I made sure I asked questions that were funny and weren't too filthy as I couldn't be bothered for more endless streams of dick pics from people I was never going to meet.

    These two rounds included "Why couldn't Timmy ride a bike?" It's because he had no legs and was a goldfish. And "Is your surname Jacobs?" That'll obviously be "Because you're a real cracker". I can't tell you which ones came from which round as men have suddenly become a lot more eager to reply. Must be because it's hot and everyone's horny, and some have even messaged me first which is very unusual.

    Here is the full list, with descriptions, of the men I'm taking into the second half of the year.

Unconventional, I know, but there's fucking loads of them and it's for my own reference as much as for yours. I may be looking for love, but after Mr Disappointment I'm not counting my chickens before they're hatched so options are necessary.

Mr Flexible

He messaged me first and the conversation to begin with was dry. He said something like "How are you sexy?" to which I replied "Sexy. Lol." I am not sexy. He disappeared for a few days then returned and it somehow moved onto number exchange. In the first few days of texting he sent me a message saying "What are you up to my baby?" MY BABY. However, as we got talking I came to realise this guy was actually hilarious, despite his inability to pick appropriate nicknames. He sent me a Snapchat of him pulling an ugly face with his leg in the air and "Much flexible. Very supple. So bendy." Written on it. I saw him walk past my bus while I was on my way home one day and he was wearing a rucksack (not in a cool way). His was officially the first arranged date of the second half and after telling me the night before that he was going to get in the bath for a long soak before a full body wax so he was "like a slippery eel" I came to the conclusion he'd at least be a character and a night in his company would certainly be entertaining.

Mr Fit Animal Man

If ever I've spoken to a man who seems impossible to work out, it's this one. And typically he's got the most beautiful face I've ever seen. He owns a parrot, two cats, two dogs, and four ferrets, and his job is looking after a wealthy family's land and animals. However he doesn't look like the type to do that at all. He looks like he'd be a big lad, dresses a bit chavvy, yet doesn't drink. He's told me he's not a people person and said he prefers animals, and at one point when I asked what kind of people he hates the most he replied with "pretentious wankers… And pakis". That was uncomfortable. I'm not sure he has very good social skills as conversation with him can be tricky, but when I back off he comes back and he texts me first every day.

I saw his profile on POF a few weeks before and fell a little bit in love with him but was too scared to send him a message, then got sad that he didn't view me back or message me. I got to 15 matches on my Tinder game a week later and then his profile came up so I broke the rule for him. It's possible I love him because he's a challenge and I can't work out if he's a player or not, but it is also possible I love him because he loves animals and I have a wonderful mental image of us growing old in a nice rustic house full of all kinds of pets and no children.

Mr Suspected Catfish

We started talking a few weeks before the end of the month and his odd behaviour quickly made me think he was a catfish. I even screenshotted his Tinder photos, emailed them to myself, and did a Google image search on that shit to see if I could find him. He asked me to send him pictures but made up a shit excuse about how he'd got a new phone four days previously and had already broken it so couldn't take pictures or send any back. I went distant and he disappeared.

A few weeks later, on my birthday to be exact, he reappeared. Spouted some rubbish about how he hadn't been in touch because he'd left his phone in a cab and was gutted he lost my number, and we started talking again. After multiple messages I decided he was actually quite sweet and following a conversation about how really romantic dates only happen in the movies he asked me out and told me he'd plan something amazing. He also said his friends told him he was doing this all wrong and he's meant to call me to arrange it, before sending me a picture that his sister told him to "send to that girl so she can see how big your nose is". The nose was the least of my worries. Not great looking, and looked about 20 years older than his Tinder photos. He also said women make him nervous which is a great start. Still, he's nice.

Mr Slow

Not overly attractive and very slow at making any kind of move but there's a lot of familiar banter, piss-taking, and I've sent him Snapchats of me pulling funny faces as it's all quite comfortable. After talking for a week and a day on Tinder I gave him my number and he reckons he was hinting for it which, if he was, I did not notice. No mention of meeting at all so I'm not sure on his intentions but will keep him going for a bit longer to see what happens as he's funny.

Mr Uni Friend

Turns out we were at the same university at the same time but our paths never crossed, which isn't too much of a surprise as he's not someone I would have been attracted to. In fact, I'm not even sure if he's someone I'd be attracted to now but he seems like a safe bet so I thought I'd see what he's about. The chat is slightly boring, no particularly funny moments or flirty behaviour. Probably won't last very long as he seems the type to potentially get a bit weird and needy. No mention of a meet.

Mr Officer

He took three days to text me after I left my number for him on Tinder. When he asked for my surname for a Facebook add and I declined as I don't want strangers stalking my whole life, he gave me a lecture about how Facebook swapping is much safer than giving strangers my number, and he is a police officer so he'd know about those things. He keeps mentioning a meeting but then disappears for days at a time so I'm not sure what kind of game he's playing. He also never Snapchats me back so he's not really playing by his own safety rules.

Mr Hairy

Very handsome man with an outstanding sense of humour. We spoke for a few days on Tinder before he went to Glastonbury and had a lot of laughs and random chat about Backstreet Boys and us getting married. I gave him my number for when he got back from the festival and he text straight away with "For when I return, in case you wonder who this weird guy texting you is." He text me upon his return and added me on Snapchat within a day.

Mr Jack

Ever seen the Robin Williams film Jack where he ages at an alarming rate? This dude is 24 but looks about 40. Seems like another safe bet with boring chat, mainly about food, and hasn't asked for my number so conversation is still on Tinder. Probably won't last long.

Mr Birthday Buddy

Celebrated his birthday around the same time as me, hence the name. Reasonably attractive, potentially short, makes no effort with conversation so I have nothing interesting to say about him as he probably won't last long either.

I'll be honest, writing them out like this disappoints me. I thought I at least had double figures but this is shit. Maybe I should start a 'refer a friend' scheme. People give me their friends to date and if one becomes my boyfriend I'll give the referee a day with my dog or something. My dog is great so that is a pretty good prize. Or maybe I could get a billboard with my face and email address on it? I need new ideas the natural search never works out for me as no one ever approaches me in person (still yet to work out why this is. Maybe I've got a funny walk or I smell musty and no one's thought to tell me. Or my life is the Truman show?! I've often suspected this), online dating clearly isn't going that well, aaand I have no other options. I'm panicking.

The Worst Date in the History of All Dating Ever

On the 1st July I was feeling positive about the new direction I'd decided on in regards to my love life, and what made it better was the fact I was seeing in the second half of the year with a date on that very day with Mr Flexible. I was fairly sure I'd figured him out to be a funny man, slightly kooky, a bit of a character, and certainly entertaining (despite the rucksack) so I was looking forward to meeting him. Unfortunately I'd forgotten rule number one of dating websites, you know jack shit about a person until you've met them in real life. A character he was, but in all the worst ways.

That lunchtime I spotted him and quickly diverted to avoid bumping into him. He was fairly chubby but wasn't walking as strangely as he had been when I saw him previously and wasn't wearing the bloody rucksack so I thought he looked alright and wasn't too nervous about meeting him. He'd imposed a communication ban until 5pm on the day and text me at 4.58pm to ask what time I'd be at the bar we were meeting in. I was trying to hang back as his office was directly opposite mine and didn't want to be awkwardly walking behind him, so when he suggested being there at 5.20pm I agreed and started walking five minutes late for good measure. It was on the walk there that he text saying "The tie has come off, it's party time". Then when I asked where he was sat he said "On the toilet crying into a pint". Strange, I thought, but it fitted in with most of the oddness he'd already come out with before this day.

    Within three seconds of walking into the bar the worst two hours of my life began. I still feel like I deserve a medal for lasting so long with this absolute creature. Upon saying hello he went straight in for a snog which I quickly avoided as we weren't familiar enough for the behaviour, so he gave me a massive cuddle and kissed me on the neck instead. Not acceptable when you've literally just met someone. He went and got me a drink before the conversation started. One of the first topics was animals and he told me all about how his cats have run away from home and he was pleased because he "fucking hates animals". He then turned his nose up and said "You've got a dog haven't you". Woah now pal, no fucker turns their nose up at my dog and gets away with it. I told him I love having a dog as he gets into bed for a cuddle in the mornings, to which he replied "I'm not sure if that's sweet or desperately sad". I'd choose him over you any day, I thought. Game over already.

Shortly after this he got up to go to the toilet and decided to give me a massage and kiss the back of my head when he came back. He did this every time he went to the toilet or to the bar which was far too often for my liking. I needed time out so excused myself and told him I was going to the toilet. As I got up to leave he said "Are you going for a little poo?" I did a confused laugh and walked off wishing I was dead.

When I returned he clearly thought this was going very well as on top of the massaging and head kissing he decided it was time to start holding my hand over the table. I think I froze temporarily unsure on how to act with this over-familiar sex pest touching me before making it seem like I needed two hands to hold my drink, and I needed my drink in my hands at all times. I then asked if his train was regular to try and hint an early finish and he came back with "As regular as your periods my darling". What? So they come constantly for one week of every month and not at all during the other three?

Not only is that a weird thing to say, but it doesn't even make sense. At least make it make sense, for fuck's sake.

Throughout the whole date so far he was also making no secret of the fact the beer was making him gassy, putting his hand in front of his mouth to do loud belches whilst animatedly blowing it to the side. Why is this guy so comfortable? This should not be happening.

We started talking about each other's voices which led him to mimic my voice whilst copying everything I said for five minutes. As if this evening could get any weirder or worse. I wanted to punch him in the face but instead I decided to pretend I needed the toilet again to get away from him. "Again?" he said, before shouting "You need to go to the toilet a lot when you've got diarrhoea don't you?" This bar was packed full of men quietly watching the football so yep, everyone heard and looked at me.

I got into the toilet cubicle and put my head on the back of the door for a minute before realising I'd gone back into polite-mode. If one person really didn't deserve common decency, it was this bellend. I went back up and without thinking put one hand on the table which of course he grabbed and tried to stroke. I snatched it away as he said "What's wrong my darling? You seem tense." OF COURSE I'M TENSE, YOU'RE FUCKING INSANE. All of his questions from this moment onwards were given the shortest answers possible. "So you don't follow sport?" "No." "None of it?" "No." "You don't even catch snippets?" "No."

He asked if I'd met anyone off Tinder before and said he'd been lucky in that none of the previous women had been crazy, "Maybe that's because I'm the weird one" he said. Probably mate. Probably. He then went on to say he'd been single for two and a half years after two serious relationships but that there had been a few women for a few months at a time in between. Seriously, if this is true it means this fucking mentalist is doing better at love than I am. Somebody shoot me.

I text my friend who lived 30 seconds away telling him I needed him to come and hold me for a minute after this shit, before panicking about the inevitable swoop towards my mouth again at goodbye. I thought that my rudeness may have told him it was a no-go but apparently not. We got outside and he did exactly what Mr Exaggerator did. He looked at my lips like he was aiming for the target. I turned my head so far it was almost backwards on my body, nearly breaking my neck as he went for the hug instead and said "Thank you so much for a lovely evening. Text me when you're home." I was at the end of my tether so simply replied with "BYE" before pacing off without looking back.

I text him when I got in anyway and decided to give him a second chance. He told me he's in love with me and suddenly I realised I love him too. We're now boyfriend and girlfriend. The end. Also I woke up this morning looking like Tina Turner.

The Man League

To keep up with the men I'm making my way through and to help those following my quest for love, I decided there was only one thing for it. A spreadsheet. Yes, I am finding love in an organised manner. Detailed within it are key things I'm looking for in my future boyfriend, including a good head of hair (very important), financially stable (no more leeches), and whether they're fucking insane or not (put simply as 'mentally stable').

There's a colour code and everything, with red being those it's game over for, amber who I'm considering, and green who I'm wet and keen for.

Speaking of being a wet, you're probably wondering about all the sex I haven't been having. I haven't had sex since Mr Disappointment. After the first week of July, the 15 week mark has been reached. I haven't had a dry patch this long since I was a virgin. Jokes, it's only since last September. But seriously, if I don't get it in soon my vagina is going to close itself up forever. The problem with wanting to be in love though is that I don't feel like I can open my legs to just anyone. Although I say this now, give me a Friday drinking date again and I'll probably be on my back quicker than a prostitute getting paid for that behaviour.

Book name	Good head of hair	GSOH	Mentally stable	Text form	Caller	Animals	Financially stable	Flirt or filth	Dares	Comments
Mr Fitness										
Mr Fit Animal Man	Yes	Reasonable	I'm going with no	Good	No	Yes	Unsure	Occasionally		Beautiful face but is also a racist and hates people. Potentially fucking insane.
Mr Slow	Reasonable	Yes	Yes	Good	No	Yes	Yes	Familiar banter	0	Very recently single. Hi I'm a rebound
Mr B Irish Boxing										
Mr Bad										
Mr Creative	Yes	Unsure	Unsure	Fair	No	Unsure	Student - unlike	Not yet	0	Told me he's had food poisoning and has spent all weekend on the toilet. Sexy
Mr Lack of Boundaries	Unsure	Yes	Unsure	Good	No	Unsure	Unsure	Not yet	0	Only started talking yesterday. Seems fun.

There really is a lot of red on that spreadsheet isn't there. I'm going to die alone, its official. Let's start with those officially out of the game.

Mr Flexible

We all know how that one went. I'd rather shit in my hands and clap than have him anything other than red.

Mr Suspected Catfish

I fear nerves may have got the better of him. He was meant to call me on a Monday but I had something come up. Tuesday after the shit date we were meant to talk but apparently he was at a conference all night. Wednesday morning I replied to his text with a long message and he simply replied with a picture of his defaced newspaper and was never heard from again. There was something weird about this guy so it's probably for the best.

Mr Uni Friend

Remember my prediction of him getting weird and needy? That happened. I got an email saying he'd viewed my Linked.in profile. Does that mean he Googled me?! Surely if you're stalking someone you don't know you're meant to make sure they don't know about it. Then he kept sending me

Snapchats of just his face and as I was the only one on his best friends list I'm guessing they were just for me, and he also screenshotted one of mine which is strange as Snapchats aren't meant to be kept. I also went to a festival in the city he lives and left early, only to wake up to a message from him saying "Why didn't you want to come and see me?" Yeah I'm going to travel an hour to see you when I don't feel well. I replied saying "Well that was never an option". He messaged again on two separate occasions to which I did not reply.

Mr Officer

Popped up on a Friday evening asking what I was doing after I'd asked him when he wanted to meet me days earlier. Surprisingly I wasn't available, asked when he's next free, and again no reply. Too flaky, he's pissing me off so can go into the red zone.

Mr Hairy

After showing so much promise he just didn't reply to my last message after continuous texting one day. Very bizarre. But his Snapchats show he's not as fit as his Tinder pictures anyway so him and his beard can go fuck themselves.

Mr Jack

Boring. Died off. Expected.

Mr Birthday Buddy

As the spreadsheet suggests, he forgot to mention he was leaving the country. Cheers for the timewasting, have a shit time.

Mr Bald

Remember him from the end of polite-mode? He came back. My men were all turning red so I thought I'd give him another go. That lasted all of two days before he tried to make me go to his house miles away and I got bored of his crap chat.

Mr Gurner

Lasted approximately two days. I replied to his message on POF, he asked for my number immediately and I was in a charitable mood so gave it to him, I then sent his pictures to my friend with a message reading "Fuck me I'm really scraping the barrel now aren't I". She called me crying with laughter which says everything. He genuinely looked like he was squeezing out a shit whilst chewing a wasp in every picture and as nice as he may be, I can't sit opposite that for an evening.

And that leads us onto the ambers. I'll be honest, this isn't going well either.

Mr Fit Animal Man

He will be red in a few days due to him being mental. He moans all the time, saying things like "Why can't everyone be dogs?" and suggests nuking the Middle East to make room for him and loads of dogs to live away from people. He also tried to have a row about big dogs being the best, and when I told him I want small dogs when I'm older he said "What a shock, a woman who wants a dog to put in her handbag. Why can't women be original?" Goes to show how little you know about me mate. I was furious; if he bothered to ask questions rather than talk about himself or dogs all the time he'd know I'm not a girl who trots around with a dog as an accessory. I take dogs very seriously, can you tell? Honestly though. God has wasted a perfectly good face on this one. He's a 23 year old man set in his ways who hates people and is too ignorant to consider anyone else's opinions. And he's on two dating websites. Good luck pal.

Mr Slow

Three weeks of talking and still no mention of meeting. I also found him on Instagram and saw lots of pictures of him with a girl, including shots of them in bed. Obviously I stalked her profile and he'd liked recent pictures of her from a week ago, and she's top on his best friends list on Snapchat (followed by me second). Obviously I asked about this and he denied it, saying they broke up a while ago and were on fairly good terms "to begin with". Why's she still at the top of your list then? Suspicious.

Mr Creative

Moved onto text fairly quickly but immediately told me he'd spent all weekend in the bathroom with food poisoning. He's not really bants either so it wasn't funny the way he said it, just a bit gross. He then spoke about how he's making a short film and when I asked what it's about he offered to send me the script. Why would I want that? Do you really think I have the time or interest to read that? Probably won't reply.

Mr Lack of Boundaries

He's chatty, interesting, reasonably funny, but keeps turning everything to sex. I'm not talking dirty with strangers anymore so will have to keep an eye on this one. His POF profile says he's 6'2" though and his pictures show he definitely isn't.

Desperate Times Call For Desperate Measures

After going HAM on Tinder at the end of June I had one real life conversion. The worst date in the world. What the fuck. My love life is like flogging a dead horse, I'm behind it desperately trying to make it move but it's not going anywhere because it's a big fucking dead horse and I have no upper body strength. I needed to do something drastic, and to get Mr Fit Animal Man and Mr Slow to pull their lazy fingers out of their arseholes to meet me.

The way I proceeded can be described as nothing short of begging. I'm not even embarrassed due to the fact I hadn't had sex in AGES and it was seriously affecting my mental and emotional wellbeing. Despite Mr Fit Animal Man's mentally unstable state I still wanted to meet him and to sit on that beautiful face, so in between his messages about hating people I suggested and pushed for an actual proper meet. He pretended to seem up for it before telling me he couldn't do much at the moment as his step-dad had just had an operation for lung cancer and his life was planned around him. He must have forgotten he'd told me his parents were going away on holiday that week so that's a fairly sick excuse. A few days later he sent me a picture of a unicorn with 'Lol I fucking hate people' written on it and I asked if that was his way of telling me he hates me. Apparently it wasn't, and he could tell I'm a "good and nice person"… but still didn't want to meet me when I said "I'm better in person". The time came to let that one die which is a damn shame but there's only so much begging a girl can do when no penis materialises.

After more social media stalking I discovered that Mr Slow's relationship was indeed over so I started pestering him to meet me too. Despite knowing he was recently single I didn't want to let go of him as easily as I did Mr Fit Animal Man as we got on so well over text and I was fairly certain that after talking for so long we'd get on just as well in person. I asked him about it outright, jested about how long we'd been talking for, and even told him it's alright if he's got a limp or a musty smell which he's embarrassed about. He said he had both of those (I think he was joking), yet still no meet was mentioned.

Mr Creative died off as he was boring me with the talk about his bowels, and Mr Lack of Boundaries was given the shove after asking if I sexted people and saying "We'll be doing it for real when we meet anyway" - gross.

As Tinder was giving me nothing but pen pals and POF was full of freaks and sex pests, I decided I needed to take it up a level. I joined Match.com. I wasn't sure if this is what people of 25 years of age do but I soon found out that plenty of 25 year olds were on there. Unfortunately they all fell into one of two categories. They were either weird and ugly, or were average looking with shit chat. God give me strength. What a waste of £40, I felt like I'd been mugged. I spoke to one who seemed to be the best of a bad bunch and gave him my number after a few messages. Bad move. I didn't reply to one message as there was nothing to comment on, and he continued to send me four messages with nothing to reply to again. "Nearly home time!" "It's Friday!" Fuck off mate, seriously. I'm not being funny, but if a girl did that to a boy she'd get bashed for being a bunny boiler or a psycho, yet men seem to get away with it all the sodding time.

I'm completely at a loss. I'm going to die alone, it's official.

Dropping Like Flies

After all the timewasters I'd put up with recently, I started making it quite clear that I wanted to meet people from the outset. A flawless system, I thought. And I was wrong. Shock.

I started talking to Mr Softly and Mr Glasses at the beginning of July and dates with both were scheduled very quickly. Mr Softly seemed like a nice boy, had good text etiquette, and replied quickly to messages. He asked if I'd like to go for a drink on the Wednesday, Thursday, or Friday of the following week but wasn't sure which one as he was in the army and would have to let me know a few hours in advance because he was so busy. This was provisionally arranged on the Sunday after about a week and a half of messaging so I waited for him to get in touch.

Mr Glasses was booked in for the Friday. He was coming from out of town to see me and we'd agreed to go for a few drinks and to see where the night took us. This date was booked in on one day, fast mover.

Wednesday rolled around and Mr Softly hadn't replied to the last message I sent on Sunday. He didn't contact me with a few hours' notice for a date, and he didn't contact me on Thursday for the same reason. In fact, he never contacted me again. My last message hadn't been particularly offensive and had followed the same pattern we'd been chatting in previously so I can only assume he simply had a change of heart and fucked off with a lack of common decency.

When talking about Friday, Mr Glasses asked what I'm looking for on Tinder and we quickly got onto the subject of people just looking for sex. He told me that wasn't what he was looking for and wouldn't arrange to have sex with someone before they met… but wouldn't turn it down should he meet someone and it was offered to which I said the same. I think this conversation may have been him subliminally trying to organise sex as he then asked if I was sure that I didn't want to go to him, and when I said no I never heard from him again either. For fuck's sake.

The concept of arranging sex before meeting someone seems so bizarre to me. It almost makes me think these people are going to be awful in real life, and they think that if you agree to shag them before you meet them you have to go through with it no matter how good or bad the date is. Imagine if I'd agreed to shag Mr Flexible before meeting him?! I probably would have jumped off a bridge swiftly afterwards. Why can't people just stop being so desperate for it and realise that this way of broaching the subject is probably going to get them nowhere? Take me out, get me drunk, and if it goes well I'll probably sleep with you no problem. But actively asking me to have sex with you based on your blurry pictures and reasonable chat is always going to be a no.

All was not lost however, as I had dates scheduled with RAF man Mr Military the following Wednesday and Dr Posh on the Friday. Mr Military was 6'3", a regular rugby player, and drove a really nice car. I'm not even materialistic but that adds to his 'looking good on paper' list. We'd been talking for about a week when it was booked in and when Wednesday came I spent the whole day psyching myself up. I was back to being nervous as he actually seemed like a normal human being which was more than what could be said for the last couple I'd met. Although there was one thing that was playing on my mind; I wasn't sure if I actually wanted to date a military man. He'd already mentioned he was going to Afghanistan next year and his shift patterns meant I'd probably only be able to see him one week out of three for the next month as my weekends were fully booked. I know it's only one date but I'm a long-term thinker, and the question of 'what if we do like each other?' is fair in my opinion.

An hour and a half before we were due to meet my worry was confirmed. The date was cancelled due to some urgent RAF business that he had to attend to. His text seemed genuine and he apologised a lot before rescheduling but my previous concerns made me realise that if we were to date, this would probably happen all the time. I don't want a part-time boyfriend and I certainly don't want to be a military wife. What if that meant I had to join that stupid choir? I hate Gareth Malone, I can't cope with that life.

The next day, Dr Posh still hadn't mentioned the date we had planned for the day after so I asked him about it. We call him Dr because he's training to be just that, and posh because he lives in a very nice town and went to a very highly regarded school. He also told me his friend had a swimming pool, sauna, steam room, and tennis courts in his house so I can't imagine he'd be riff raff if he associates himself with those kinds of people. Dr Posh often took a long time to reply which was a shame as had he been more constant he probably would have been my favourite. He had a good sense of humour, we seemed to get on quite well, and for our first date we were meant to be travelling out to a bigger city to meet for cocktails.

When I mentioned it he took hours to reply and his message back told me he had to work the next day due to being insanely busy. He asked if he could let me know but I didn't want to take a change of clothes to work, psyche myself up all day, for it to be cancelled yet again so I suggested a reschedule. He said "Yes ok, I do 100% want to do it still" and asked if I have every weekend off, which I told him I do without informing him I have no weekend time free for the next month. No date was mentioned yet the occasional text is still dripping in.

Mr Slow had recently had a change of heart. After five weeks of not arranging a meet he's arranged three dates for next week with me. Presumptuous and odd but still quite nice. I'm not sure what's gotten into him to make him so keen all of a sudden, it could be that he jokingly set my picture as his phone background and his mates saw it, could be that he hasn't had sex in a while, or could be that he's realised I'm not going to leave him alone until he meets me so has given in. Either way, if recent rendezvous' are anything to go by I'll be expecting three pies on all three days next week as he'll probably fucking cancel as well.

Dating in the summer is shit. I wonder if it's the heat putting people off. Thinking about a sweaty post-sex spoon when it's muggy as hell isn't a great thought, or maybe they don't have any reasonable dating attire suited to the weather. It could be because summer is just a busy time of year and everyone's too busy having fun with all their plans and their mates to want to meet someone. Roll on the darker nights and cooler temperatures, I bet they'll all be fucking scrambling for their winter wifey when that comes around.

The End of a Slow Summer

A few days of shit chat and Mr Military died off. The rescheduled date was never carried out and he was gone for good. Leading up to my holidays I decided to refrain from finding any new meat as I had no time to meet them and I couldn't be arsed to talk to people about how their days have been for weeks before a date because, to be honest, I don't give a shit how these peoples' days are when I've never even met them.

Mr Slow was still on the go and the three dates were still scheduled until the day before when I cancelled as I remembered I had an essay due and had no time spare for him whilst rushing to get it done. The following week, after seven weeks and two days of talking, we finally met.

The Friday before I had drunk dialled him and it was after this conversation that I started wondering whether I would actually fancy him. He'd made references to his weight and in some pictures he looked fairly chubby, but on the phone he seemed young and the combination of it was starting to put me off. It may have also been the fact I'd had enough of men but I went to meet him all the same as after such a long time it had to be done.

He told me during our drunken phone chat that he'd bought a whole new outfit for his first ever first date with me and he turned up wearing just that. Chinos, shoes, a white t shirt and a blazer. None of it fit properly as he was indeed chubby and also short which meant he didn't carry it well. I know it sounds awful but clothes that don't fit right are such a turn off for me. I want to know you're mentally old enough to be able to dress yourself and don't need to be told by your mum that your sleeves are too long and your belly is on show through your t shirt. Within seconds of greeting him I already knew it wasn't going to happen.

The conversation flowed well during dinner once he'd stopped sweating from the walk to the restaurant and I quickly realised he was much more of a raging lad than I'd previously thought. I'd been hoodwinked by the perfect spelling and grammar in his texts and assumed he seemed older than his age, but sitting opposite him in his baggy blazer with chewing gum in his mouth all through dinner because he had nowhere to put it there wasn't any hint of sexual chemistry. It was because of this lack of spark I thought it was alright to convince him to show me his party trick: downing a whole pint in three seconds. Not the classiest of dates but an experience to have witnessed nonetheless.

The whole date was just a bit meh. There was nothing of particular interest to note apart from the fact I worried the whole way through about whether or not he was going to try and kiss me. I really really didn't want him to do that. And so, when it came to saying goodbye at the train station I lit a cigarette just before and edged away slowly after a brief hug and thanks.

He text me the next day and chat continued until the day after: the day before I was due to go on holiday. And when I got to my hotel I made the decision not to text him back, so I didn't ever again. Probably quite harsh considering the length of time we'd been talking but Instagram stalking told me he had another option on the go who he'd taken for a night time stroll on the beach the night after our date so I didn't feel too guilty. Had he double text I'd have let him down gently, but he didn't so there was no need. I debated keeping him going for the sake of getting some sex but then I thought he probably wouldn't be able to keep up with me and it wouldn't be very good so there was no need to take it any further.

Just before my holiday I had an unexpected return. Mr Fit Animal Man came back after I drunkenly included him in a Snapchat round whilst away the weekend before meeting Mr Slow. He asked if I was up for meeting soon and we agreed to arrange something after my holiday despite my shock of him even suggesting it. We spoke every day and after my date with Mr Slow we ended up exchanging semi-naked photos. A few gins and apparently I think I'm some kind of porn star, when really I'm wearing massive pants and am surrounded by a tip of a room. Sexy. For some reason it was also arranged for us to send each other a picture a day while I was away and so it continued. I even managed to get in a bikini shot as the lighting in the bedroom made my gunt look significantly smaller than it does in real life which I was quite pleased about.

On the last day of my holiday he went quiet again. I sent him a picture in the evening, he replied, I replied, then he didn't again until the next day. I was pissed off as he seems to play hot and cold all the time and is probably a lot more effort than he's worth. Quite frankly, he's a fucking idiot and if that day hadn't confirmed it then the conversation we had a few days later did.

I didn't text him to say I'd landed and two days later he asked if I'd made it back safely. Talk then got onto us meeting and I realised he still had the idea in his head of me going all the way to his house for the night of our first meet. He's not mentally stable enough for me to feel comfortable with that. I tried to budge him and there was no movement so I told him it's time to call it a day. He came back with some shit like "I won't tell you the reason I won't go out as I don't think it'll help my case. I guess I just have to accept the fact this is ending and leave you to find someone more suited." Bullshit, absolute bullshit. I simply responded with "Ok" rather than asking what his excuse is because I know it's nothing but laziness.

Here's some of the theories that were mentioned and denied amongst friends:

- **Police tag and curfew.** Nope, he went out for dinner a couple of days before and my social media stalking showed that he often goes to gigs.

- **Recluse or doesn't like crowds.** Nope. For reasons mentioned above and also he goes to watch football very often.

- **He's disabled.** Unlikely as he has a fairly active job and plays a lot of football.

Another man who just wanted sex to walk through his front door. Piss off.

During my holiday I made a decision. I'm going back to being a player. Looking for love is so stressful and depressing and I'm quite sure it's never going to happen. Also I still haven't had sex since Mr Disappointment and I think I'm finally back to the mental state where I can have sex with people I don't fancy very much. I've got a wide on for winter and I'm confident the cock will come calling now the nights are drawing in. Positive mental attitude my friends, positive mental attitude for penis.

Fucked Over by Karma

Shortly after writing the previous chapter I had my first post-summer date and yes, karma fucked me over. Remember when I said I'm back in the mental state where I can sleep with people I'm not attracted to? I was proved horribly wrong.

      I arranged to meet this one on a Tuesday evening outside a coffee shop before going for a drink. I had no particular feeling towards him beforehand apart from that he was so hideously average I couldn't be bothered to go at all. There was no flirty banter, no compliments, just constant mundane shit chat. I started regretting this quest for sex a bit at that point as well. The end of the year needs to be epic to make the book go out with a bang but I'm shit at dating because I'm a naturally miserable cunt. I can't be arsed to sit and listen to these people talk about themselves for an evening as I don't care what they do or what they like, and I certainly can't be arsed to talk about myself to people I'm never going to see again. I don't even find myself interesting enough to talk about for a few hours, let alone another person. Dating isn't fun, it's shit.

Having said that, I am incredibly good at pretending I'm having a good time and faking an interest, and exceptional at remembering the details and conversations from ten different men at one time so I suppose if anyone's the woman for the job it's me.

As I approached my date for the evening I saw him sat outside the coffee shop. I waved and rather than start walking towards me he stayed seated and waited for me to make the awkward walk right up to where he was. He looked at me for a second before jumping up, shaking my hand, kissing me on the cheek and introducing himself. It was at this moment I realised he almost definitely had special needs. His mannerisms were jittery, his facial expressions looked like he was gurning, and he stammered on everything he said. God give me strength. I went to the toilet immediately upon entering the bar of choice and tried not to smash my face on the wall in anticipation of spending an evening with Mr Special.

The conversation was as boring as could be expected covering shit like work, hobbies and interests, and the basic home life and background information. However, I couldn't look directly at him through any of this because when he wasn't gurning he was rolling his eyes over my whole body like he'd never sat so close to a woman before and was imagining me naked. Trying not to cringe or cry was one of the toughest tasks I've ever lived through in my meagre 25 years on this earth.

After an hour and a half and two drinks down he returned from a toilet break and headed to the bar to get in the next round. I couldn't sit through another one and had to cut it short, making an excuse about being tired and having to be up for work in the morning. It was 9.30pm and as strange as he was, I don't think he quite bought it. He still tried his luck as we said goodbye though. We got to the point where our paths parted and I gave him a polite hug. Rather than putting his hands in a place that's suitable following a first meeting with someone who clearly wasn't sexually attracted to him, he placed one hand on the small of my back and the other firmly on my arse. Not appropriate.

I left after saying "see you… erm… soon maybe" and held in my laughter from the shock of the groping as I half-ran out of his vicinity before getting to a safe place to call my friend and howl in awkward amusement as I retold the story of the evening at the bus stop.

He text me later on thanking me for going out to meet him and said he had "a lovely time" then text me again the following day asking how I was. Both texts were ignored. I fear that having sex with someone with special needs would not only make my readers like me a bit less, but would also cause me to have some kind of breakdown about the state of my life in light of shagging people like him for entertainment purposes. Also he groped away any feelings of pity I may have had so I feel like my ignoring was completely justified.

Fucked Over by Karma (Part 2)

When I first got a message from Mr Train Driver I refrained from mentioning we'd already exchanged a few words earlier in the year but it had dried up fairly quickly. On his profile he'd painted himself as a quirky indie type with face fuzz, floppy hair, artsy tattoo shots and diving pictures. He also had something along the lines of "I've changed this to 'looking to date but nothing serious' as I'm going to Thailand for seven weeks in October. I'm looking for friends and maybe more when I get back, basically I'm not just looking for a quick shag. But if things do go well obviously accommodation will be free with me in Thailand in my apartment." Slightly strange statement to make, I thought. Seven weeks isn't that long mate.

We chatted, he was pleasant, and I gave him my number fairly quickly. The texting was lengthy and constant (just how I like my penises) and he seemed nice. Just nice. He wrote "Ha!" at the end of almost every sentence which I found really fucking irritating but the good spelling and grammar and ability to hold a conversation made me stick with it.

If I'm honest, I was probably a little bit of a cunt during the pre-date text stages. He once offered to send me the link of a diving video from last time he'd been away and rather than enthusiastically saying yes then telling him how great it was, my reply was "No thanks, I don't like fish." Blunt. One weekend I was on a night out and the day before he was asking if he'd be getting any drunken texts. At this point I was talking to about ten different men so my main thought process was 'as if he thinks this is going well enough for that'. After sending a Snapchat that night to him and many other men, he also text saying "No drunk texts last night but you did send a Snapchat! Don't worry it wasn't anything revealing but you did look very pretty!" Pfff pretty, what a pussy there was cleavage in there and everything. And he thinks that was just for him, what a mug.

We arranged to go for a drink on a Tuesday night at a pub round the corner from me and he tried insisting beforehand on picking me up and dropping me off. Yes, please come along to my council flat and get me will you? Say hello to Mental Gail who lives opposite while you're here, she's bound to stick her head in the window of your car anyway. I've become very precious about this as you may be able to tell. I don't care that I live in a council flat I tell friends, colleagues and anyone who's reading this. Most people give it the old "Oh don't be silly!" but seriously, if you were chatting to someone you met on a dating site before meeting and they said "I live in a council flat" you'd make an assumption. Not having any of that thanks.

When I was getting ready I had my usual meltdown of 'I can't fucking be arsed. I hate people I just want to sit at home with my dog. I'm so bored of generic date chat, I don't give a shit what he does for work or fun, I don't want to hear about his family, why can't we just get wasted and have sex'. Regardless of this, I got dressed and dragged myself down the road anyway and was about ten minutes late before spotting him lurking by the entrance.

What happened next was very surprising. He was so much more attractive in real life than in pictures; tall, rugged, had a real sexy voice, looked straight in my eyes and charmed me like a fucking snake. I was smitten within about ten minutes, what the fuck. We sat down with our drinks and chatted. There was no generic date chat, no talk of work apart from taking the piss out of colleagues and customers, and talk of family but only the interesting stuff. The conversation flowed like we'd known each other for ages. I was actually enjoying myself; we were having a laugh and he mentioned a few things that gave me a slight throb on. Made it clear he could dance, tick, spoke about djing, tick, laughed at my jokes, tick, was also a smoker, tick. Just tick tick tick fucking tick. This was the best date I'd had all year by a country mile.

    The date was cut fairly short on account of him having to be up at 5am the next day for work. I let him drop me to the end of my road and as we pulled up we had a hug (still never sure whether to go for a snog) and gave it the old "lovely to meet you" business. He then said "I'm off next Tuesday and Wednesday" and I looked at him unsure of how to proceed. HE WANTS TO SEE ME AGAIN?! It was a miracle. I got a good one and he's considering the thought of sticking his dick in me. What a great day. It was then arranged that we'd go to the cinema on the Wednesday as he was yet to see The Inbetweeners 2. I got out of the car and skipped all the way home.

    Mr Train Driver text me when he got in asking how my bed felt, thanking me again for the evening, and telling me about his journey home. A few more messages were exchanged before the goodnights and the smile plastered across my face stuck for about 24 hours. It was at around the 24 hour mark when this smile started to waiver. Hadn't fucking heard from him all day had I. Typical. During the pre-date text stage I usually heard from him every other day so I wasn't too worried as we had another date planned anyway. Thursday came. Didn't hear from him again. Friday came. Guess what happened!... Nope, didn't hear from him.

I was out with work having a few end of week drinks and decided to bite the bullet. I was committing the cardinal sin of the double text. I convinced myself it was alright as the last message on Tuesday had just been saying goodnight but I still didn't feel alright about it. He replied instantly to my "Hiii how are you? Good week?" I punched the air and text back with standard chat then told him I was having a few drinks. "Enjoy your night!" he replied. Is that it?! For fuck's sake. Bye then, prick. I left it until the next day before replying and deliberately put no questions and referenced his days off to see what he said. I'll tell you what he said… Nothing. He said absolutely nothing and I never heard from him ever again.

Why in shit's name would you arrange a second date with someone if you have no intention of seeing them again? Did he think I'd just forget he existed and never question the fact he just fucking disappeared?! Seriously, I'm a big girl and I won't cry myself to sleep if you just say "See you around" or "Speak soon" or just fucking "BYE".

I've got a few theories about this one. Allow me to explain:

• **The Thailand thing.** That's fair. But it's ONLY SEVEN WEEKS. And why bother going on a date if you don't want to meet someone before?

• **He's just a good date.** I now consider myself a good date after all this practice. At the beginning of the year I was shit. I had no idea what I was doing, no idea what to talk about, got nervous, said the wrong things. He had also been on POF for ages which I know due to the earlier messages and always seeing his profile. Maybe he too is just very well practiced and that's the reason we got on so well, opposed to any real chemisty.

• **He thought I was ugly.** Always an option.

• **Doesn't know what he wants.** The length of time he's been on there suggests he could just be really fussy with a set checklist he wants a woman to have. He'd said he wasn't after a quick shag on his profile and none of his chat or behaviour said he was lying about that.

- **Grass is greener syndrome.** He'd been liking pictures of another girl on Instagram which I thought may have been another potential option. Her page was open and was full of pictures of spliffs. Such employability.

Either way, this is karma getting me for pieing off so many men after the first date this year and for saying 'I never get pied off anymore'. Anyway, I'm over it…

And I hope he has a shit time in Thailand.

The End of the Dry Spell

When I first saw Mr Kid on Tinder I couldn't decide whether he was attractive or not. He looked like he had potential but there was something about his face that was a bit strange. After ten seconds of debating I decided his face intrigued me so I swiped right and low and behold, we had a match.

      He started the best way anyone ever has, by asking me if I ever just sit and think about where milk comes from and how it was discovered. This genuinely is something that troubles me regularly; it was like he'd seen into my soul and figured out how weird I am immediately. We got on exceptionally well and were exchanging long messages all day long. This guy seemed cool, I was happy with this one. We'd planned three dates before even meeting as he suggested me going to his and him cooking for me but I said a public meet would probably be more appropriate for date one, and when he mentioned he worked in a bar out of town in a place I'd never been we agreed that's where we'd go for a picnic on date three.

Somehow, we started a question and answer game to get to know each other. Everything asked was fairly safe and there were no hints at filth but I just put it down to him being a normal person and not a massive sex pest like most of the other men I came into contact with. One of the questions I asked was "When's your birthday?" and followed it with "You're 24 aren't you?" as that's what his Tinder had said. His reply was "No… Is that what my profile says?" I panicked. Then, rather than telling me his age he sent a screenshot of what his profile said on his end. 19. FUCKING NINETEEN. Six years my junior, I'm such a groomer. He followed this with "I hope this doesn't change things because I think you're great." By this point we'd already been talking a week and at no point had I had a feeling he was younger than me so after the initial shock I got over it and YOLO'd on, thinking shagging someone barely out of puberty would at least be an experience.

We met two days after Mr Train Driver pied me off and went for dinner and drinks after work. I say after work, I mean after I finished work. He was a student at the local university. Of course he was. On first impression when meeting him I was fairly pleased. He was so thin though, I spent most of the time mentally picturing me climbing on top of him naked and him snapping in half then the police banging my door down for paedophilia and murder.

One thing I did notice about him during this date was that he liked talking about himself a lot. I could barely get a word in edgeways and when I did he continued to talk about himself like he knew everything at the age of 19. Also he was a massive snob and clearly had a very comfortable family; there was no chance I could ever bring him round to my council flat. He spoke about the standard girls from my town like they were all gobby slags (probably not an unfair generalisation, hi) and went on about people he worked with who were scummy and poor.

Regardless of this, I'd had a good enough time to know I could tolerate sleeping with him. At the end of the date he asked if I'd enjoyed the evening and if I was still up for him cooking. I said yes and he proceeded to snog me at the bus stop before saying goodbye. I won't lie; it was a real good kiss. He cupped my chin and bent down, there was no slobber, just enough tongue, and nice soft lips. I was throbbing the whole way home thinking about it. It was like a sensational icing on top of a cake that had been left out uncovered all day, edible but a little bit dry.

We had some texts when I got in and the next day when I asked if he had much on that week he said "No, when are you free?" Very keen indeed. Looks like someone's getting it in soon I thought, as I fist pumped to celebrate. He had work on Friday and Saturday but didn't start until 10pm so we agreed I'd go round on the Saturday. However, as the week progressed and the day approached I was less than keen. I kept thinking about his self-importance when we first met and couldn't think of anything worse than spending an evening listening to him going on. I was also recovering from a stinking cold so had no motivation to do anything.

I dragged myself out of bed, shaved my muff, and took a shot of Man the Fuck Up before getting the bus and trudging to his house. I was running slightly late as usual and text him to tell him this, worried about the fact he'd started cooking. "Not to worry, dinner's on a slow cook in the oven" he replied. How bizarre, I don't think I've ever met a man who would slow cook a meal. Or even one who's wanted to cook for me before come to think of it. This wasn't your average 19 year old boy.

When I arrived he told me to take a seat in the living room before cracking open a bottle of his favourite pinot grigio. A wine drinker as well, and a picky one at that. We sat watching TV whilst sitting next to, but not touching, each other on the sofa. Dinner was served. It was a big heaped plate of pasta with a cheesy, meaty sauce and meatballs. Definitely not thrown together, made from scratch and with plenty of seasoning. A proper little chef. It was lovely but I barely touched it as I still wasn't feeling great and I worried it would give me wind which isn't ideal when a shagging was probably a couple of hours away. Also, the heat of the plate was making my face sweat immensely and I already felt a bit tipsy from the wine so I thought it best to call it a day before all of my make-up had completely slid off my face and he didn't want to stick it in me anymore.

Seeing him in his natural environment, he was visibly more relaxed than he had been during date one and I liked him a lot more this time round. We were having a laugh, taking the piss out of each other, and he seemed a lot more human than the uptight boy I'd met previously. It almost felt like we were a couple having a cosy Saturday night in at one point.

Dessert was served in the form of a massive bar of chocolate. He had all bases covered, I wonder what else he's prepared I thought. We were starting to run out of time for a proper session when he gradually started moving in. First he let our legs touch, then his hand rested on my lap for a while, and then he finally went in for the kiss. Things started getting steamy on the sofa but his deeply religious housemate was in and I really didn't want to be caught naked and full of cock by a God-loving child so the suggestion to take it upstairs was made.

We trailed up and as I went in I noticed his room was spotless and his bed made perfectly. Someone was expecting a bedroom visitor. He got on top of me with the lights still on full and I told him to turn them off before clothes started coming off. The sex was a solid 7.5 out of 10, surprising for someone so young but he knew how to work a woman better than some men much his senior I'd experienced in the past.

He knew about foreplay and warmed me up nicely before the main event started and clothes weren't even off in their entirety when it began which added to the excitement of it. His trousers were just slightly pulled down and I still had my bra and dress on as he mounted me. Mr Kid then turned me over and doggy styled me but I did have to stop myself from laughing when his spanking was resembled a man herding cattle rather than anything sexy. All clothes were off by the time I followed his request and "got on top to fuck him".

As he was almost done, he tried to finish me off before making me lose my flow by asking "where do you want me to come?" What a question. As I had to get the bus home and didn't fancy sitting in public with semen dripping off my face I told him to do it inside me as it seemed like the most reasonable place. "In your fanny?" FANNY. What a horrible word to use during sex. But yes, Kid, in there. He stuck it in, didn't pump, and didn't make any noise. In fact he didn't make any noise at all throughout it apart from for the two seconds when I put it in my mouth. I did go to kiss him as he entered though and his mouth was violently open so I assumed he'd done it. When it was all over he said "thank you, that was very nice" before asking if I wanted any tissue and reaching down beside the bed to pick up a toilet roll. Amazing. This one must be the most detailed man I've ever met.

He had to go straight to work dripping with sweat and smelling like sex while I strolled back to the bus leaking his man deposit in my knickers. I followed this session by going home, having a rinse, and getting on my gladrags on for a night out with the girls. They were already out and I was met by them cheering "WEEEYYY" and high fives all round. Lads.

When we'd departed he kissed me and said "I'll see you soon" before texting me thanking me for the evening and reiterating the "see you soon" again.

Over the next two days his text game had dramatically decreased. He text me first on both days but no questions were asked, there was little attempt at creating any kind of conversation, and when I asked if he had much on that week he made no suggestion to see me again. I bit the bullet on the Monday and asked if he wanted to do something on the Wednesday and he agreed saying he'd plan a surprise. How exciting. The Tuesday came around and no texts were exchanged either way. I wasn't too worried as we'd be seeing each other the next day but when I text to confirm plans after not hearing from him he replied with "Sorry hun I forgot I have to work tonight, are you free tomorrow?" Tomorrow was confirmed before I remembered his work was only open on Friday and Saturday nights. Looks like I won't be 'seeing him soon' after all I thought. Fucking annoying as I wasn't thrilled about breaking my streak of shagging every 2014 man twice for the first time in my life.

He didn't get in touch to confirm plans the next day either but on the Saturday of that week I did notice he'd added me on Snapchat. That night I was going out and looked sexy so I added a selfie to my Snapchat Story as an indirect 'fuck you child' signal before putting the same picture on a Tinder moment to make sure he knew I was still active on there too. I thought it was game over but they always come back, and that he did.

The Night of Realisations

Two days after the indirect Snapchat dig at Mr Kid I went for dinner with a friend to catch up on all recent happenings. As we always do, we started by exchanging our man stories to fill the other in on what had been going on.

One of the stories I told was of Mr Train Driver and his disappearing act. Turns out my friend knows him, and not for good reasons. He used to go out with a friend of hers and turned out to be a compulsive liar and a massive player. Who'd have bloody thought it. Although shocked, I couldn't help but have wished he'd attempted to play me so I'd have at least got a shag out of the situation. What a load of shit. Not even good enough for him to chuck and fuck, I hate my life.

We also sat and discussed all of the reasons for Mr Kid pieing me off. I'm not shit at sex so it can't be that, even if he was silent for most of it. I told her all about the theories me and other friends had thrown out but we were still none-the-wiser, as no one ever is when someone suddenly disappears on them.

On the way home, four days after we were meant to be going on our third surprise date, Mr Kid text me. What I read left me speechless. What I read also confirmed one of the many theories me and my friend had settled on. The text read exactly like this…

"Sorry I haven't text in a few days I've been in the country. You are a lovely girl and I feel so bad for doing this. But the reason I haven't seen you again is not you it's me. I have fallen for a boy. I didn't mean it to happen we were friends and it's just happened."

Holy fucking shitballs. A few things. Firstly; "it's not you it's me" as if you just used that line. Also it is me a bit as I can't grow a penis and I'm sorry about that. Secondly; "it's just happened", since when does suddenly being a homosexual just happen? At least he called me a lovely girl, that makes me feel much better as it confirms the only reason for getting rid of me is my gender.

Some of you may be questioning the authenticity of this message. However, there are some facts about him I missed out previously and which I overlooked during the dates as my brain was being led by my vagina.

- The bar he works in is a gay bar.

- All of his friends are gay.

- He's incredibly camp.

- Remember when he cooked for me?

- Remember when I said he only drinks pinot grigio? Penis grigio more like. Hold the grigio.

- He got very offended when I made a joke about him being gay, even though he was sat there singing 'In the Navy'.

- Aaaand the fact that HE CLEARLY LOVES COCK.

I'm not unfamiliar with this kind of man. When I was young and at uni I knew of many who saved it until their student years to come out. However, back in those days I wasn't used for my husky voice to try and keep them on the straight and narrow. I have been the subject of a child's attempt to stick to fanny and I failed. Still, at least I'm a lovely girl.

    I didn't reply to his text as much as I did respect his honesty. I wasn't quite sure what to say, should I have congratulated him on coming out and wished him and his boyfriend a happy life together? Having sex with a gay child was never something I envisioned when this year began but on the plus side I haven't yet been arrested as part of Operation Yewtree and he lived through the episode of my hefty body fucking his tiny frame so we'll put it down to experience and move onto the next chapter.

The Big Dicked Perv

Mr Big Dicked Perv first made contact in May through Tinder. We had a couple of messages before it died out and a week or so later he sent me another message asking for my Snapchat username. Fairly harmless I thought, so I gave it to him. However, it soon became apparent he wasn't asking to add me so he could exchange friendly face snaps and in came a barrage of pictures and videos of him playing with his penis. His fucking enormous penis at that.

    We had a few more messages where he asked me to send filthy pictures back and tried to insinuate dirty talk but I called him a perv and told him there was no way I was partaking in any behaviour of the sort. I asked him if he actually met anyone off Tinder and he told me he was 'waiting on something else' and just got off on knowing loads of random girls are watching him wank himself off. At least he's honest.

    He went quiet for months and reappeared at the beginning of October. Clearly this one he'd been waiting on had enough of him and he was back to entertaining strangers with his massive penis.

It was around this time that I realised how desensitised I'd become to the world of online dating and the sex pests that lurked there. This time I didn't tell him to piss off and turn my nose up at his filth, I engaged. He did ask me to send videos of me using my rabbit but I wasn't quite there yet. Tit pictures and the chat, however, was on. I was in love with that massive penis of his, I couldn't stop thinking about how big it was and how I wanted it smashed straight into my uterus. After having the dry spell broken by Mr Kid I was dangerously close to humping the legs of passers-by as the horn was stronger than ever and I desperately needed a good seeing to.

I asked him when he was coming to my hometown as he lived a couple of hours away and he'd agreed on the following weekend. Of course that weekend came around and he'd gone quiet for a few days so never had any intention of actually shagging me. He was still simply enjoying making girls up and down the country moist at the sight of his weapon.

I'd become a girl who was happy to consent to sex before meeting someone, and when I'm in this way and my vagina rules my thinking only bad things can happen. Nine solid months of online dating is unhealthy, my mind has been completely changed about the values of love and sex and I just want to get it in 24/7.

The Week of Shit Men

The Monday after being boned by Mr Kid I met Mr Pasty for a drink. His pictures had been a bit blurry and he'd been blonde which wasn't usually my bag but he had real good chat and was very entertaining via text so I had high hopes for it being a reasonably good evening. We were originally scheduled to meet the week before but he'd mentioned it was the day before payday and his bank balance looked dire which made me wince slightly as we know I'm not a fan of the money talk but my hangover meant I couldn't stomach meeting him a for a drink anyway. So I changed our date to a day after payday - a day I knew I definitely wouldn't have to fund.

He drove over my way so I didn't have to get a bus anywhere and we went to a local bar, not realising it was pub quiz night. During the getting ready stages I couldn't be bothered and my stomach was doing the usual churn, although I knew I'd been fine once I got there as I always am. Being such an experienced dater by now meant that there were no nerves once I was in someone's company and it was only the before bit that had me shitting and heaving thanks to my IBS not being able to handle the thought of spending an evening with a stranger.

Mr Pasty offered to pick me up which I obviously declined and I stood waiting for him to arrive. When I spotted him I wasn't disappointed but I wasn't particularly excited either, so I hit neutral and behaved as I would around any other person. He did not follow suit and was clearly quite nervous. I don't have the patience or the enthusiasm to deal with this.

He asked if I'd eaten and if I wanted to get any food while we were there to which I said no. I asked if he was hungry and he told me he'd been grazing on buffet food all day at work due to it being someone's birthday so he was alright. I was constantly reminded of this through the evening as every ten seconds I got a waft of pasty where he'd clearly done a silent burp from his position in front of me.

Conversation didn't flow and he seemed to be struggling to think of what to say. Instead of keeping the talk going he just kept looking at me with a strange and slightly awkward smile on his face. This wasn't going well. I thought if nothing else he'd at least be an easy evening date but his behaviour was throwing me off my usual flow; staring straight at me, pasty burps and the weird laugh that kept coming out of him every time I said anything. His head would go forward like a chicken and some deep pneumatic chortle would fall out of him. So off-putting.

After each of us buying a drink he asked if I wanted another one. I said no and made up some rubbish about being tired before he offered a lift home, or even for him to walk me there. Another no and an awkward hug later and I was gone.

I considered keeping him going for a week after for the sake of a potentially good chapter but I then realised the thought of having sex with him made me feel a bit sick and that I'd have to be smashed to let him inside me. The following weekend he also started the talk of how he was skint as his bank account had been rinsed on another night out so I pied him off by ignoring him as I always do. A couple of messages later and he gave up which was nice and easy. There was nothing interesting about him and our meeting had just been another night full of standard boring date talk which had added to my dislike of him. The chance of him being entertaining was obviously a bad call on my part.

That Friday, and adding to my lack of will for boring men, I met Mr Unimpressed. We'd been talking on and off for a few weeks and had finally arranged to meet for a drink. I couldn't work him out from his messages but my Facebook stalk suggested he was a bit of a lad and quite attractive so I thought there might have been a Friday treat in the form of his penis in store after a night on the lash.

On the way there he text me telling me he'd let me know when he was parking. Sorry, what? Driving? It's a fucking Friday night! I called him a lightweight and he asked if we could meet 15 minutes later so he could get the train. I agreed despite this meaning I'd be waiting for half an hour as I hadn't got dressed up and sacrificed a Friday night for a couple of drinks and a polite kiss on the cheek goodbye. I sat and chain smoked and people watched whilst waiting for him which got dull fairly quickly. I wanted a drink and was starting to wish I'd just stayed at home as this was the worst beginning to a date ever. I tried to convince myself it might actually turn out to be the best date ever as I watched what could have been my bus home pull away and went to stand outside the train station's entrance to meet him.

I thought I spotted him but was glad when that guy walked past, then thought I'd spotted him again and was even gladder when that one went another way in the station as well. Third time lucky I thought. Oh no. The second guy came back and as he came closer I realised it was definitely him. Clearly he's very photogenic, I thought, and he was no taller than 5'7" which I wasn't keen on. He saw me, I said hello, he said hello, and then without taking his eyes off me he carried on walking past. What the fuck. I had to chase him; he kissed me on the cheek whilst still continuing to walk on, and made some small talk seeming completely unimpressed by me the whole time. He even had the cheek to say "at least I recognised you" when clearly he hadn't, or if he had he was just making himself look like even more of a rude bastard.

For the second date this week the talk was strained. There were a lot of awkward pauses as he had nothing to say and frankly I couldn't be bothered to entertain this bellend for a whole evening when he'd made it clear within seconds that he wasn't mad about the idea of spending time with me. It was after the second drink; the doubles round which I had bought in an attempt to get pissed hoping the evening would get better, that he asked what time my bus was. We'd been sat there for an hour and I sat with an empty glass for a further 30 minutes as he admitted he'd driven to the train station on the other end and didn't want another one.

We took a quiet walk back to the station where he gave me the obligatory hug goodbye (wish he hadn't) and I stood and smoked three fags whilst trying to locate some friends so my aesthetic efforts for the evening hadn't completely gone to waste. This too was unsuccessful as my phone died and I trudged into a taxi rather than waiting 20 minutes fuming for the bus. The taxi driver was the only good thing about the evening as he asked me all about my love life and told me being married is shit and boring anyway.

No texts were exchanged between me and Mr Unimpressed unsurprisingly, but at least I had a night out the following day to look forward to. Maybe I'd defeat The Week of Shit Men and find a man organically through natural search. Maybe, just maybe.

Our First Organic Man

I got dressed up for my night out and if I'm honest, I looked great. I felt great too and had one goal in mind. Cock. It was going to be an evening hunt of epic proportions and I wasn't going home alone, I was going to make sure of that.

    Two bottles of Prosecco between two of us meant I was already smashed before moving onto our last destination of the evening. I was like a whirlwind, talking to every man I could get my hands on and had already snogged two and seen one of their penises after he cracked it out in the smoking area to prove it was massive within a few hours of being in the venue.

    I'm not sure how my final victim came about. We had a mutual friend so our groups were kind of merged towards the end of the night and my fuzzy memory can only remember kissing him once before talk of where we lived came about and how living with our families meant we'd have to get a hotel. We left fairly quickly after this and made our way down the road to the cheapest hotel in town stumbling along the way as we were both as battered as each other.

He was fairly attractive, had a thick head of hair, and that's about as much as I saw when I pounced on him it would seem. We rang the front bell of the hotel as the doors were locked and asked if we could get a room when the man on reception came to let us in. After he'd paid £65 and we were given our key card it took us about half an hour to actually get into the room. We weren't aware that the key card also had to be swiped in the lift so on three occasions we got in, pressed the button, and ended back where we started. Our drunken confusion wasn't quite registering what was happening and in the end the reception man had to take us up himself. We probably should have just been sent home at this point, that would have been the best option for everyone.

When we got into the room clothes came off quickly and I realised at this point he was a lot fatter naked than he looked when covered. I've turned into the world's biggest hypocrite. I'm fat but I don't like the look of a fat man. Something about it just doesn't sit well with me. Regardless of this I was obviously going to shag him anyway as we'd come this far, so we got into bed and he got moving on the foreplay.

He wasn't good at this, he was rough with his hands, lacked rhythm and the too-short stubble meant it felt like my vagina was having a fight with sandpaper while he was going down on me. After a long time of this I wondered why he hadn't made the appropriate move and shoved it in yet. Reaching around I tried to find his cock to reciprocate the pre-sex activities to lead into getting it in. 'Tried to find' being the key words in this instance. I finally found it. It was fucking tiny. I had gone home with Mr Tiny Penis Man. And on top of that, he couldn't even get an erection. What a fucking waste of time.

All of what had happened so far had been quite sobering so by this point I was fully aware of what was going on. Despite this, I agreed to his request and put his tiny flaccid penis in my mouth to try and make it work. It was like putting a finger in my mouth and my entire being cringed as I attempted to suck something that was barely there. It didn't work and it certainly wasn't going to so when he said "but I want to fuck you" (probably wouldn't even be able to do that with an erection anyway) I suggested trying in the morning. He tried once more to make me come with his hands but I'm not a faker and obviously he failed as he had done for the past few hours, even when I tried to lead him in the right direction, so we gave up and he spooned me naked as we went to sleep. I wish he hadn't done that either.

In the morning I was awoken by him trying again. The sight of his hungover face trying to be sexy on top of me didn't exactly put me in the mood and yet again that tiny penis of his wasn't moving. It was still early so I kind of rolled out and had my back to him when he reached under and started fingering me. I thought trying to get the act done was the best idea as at least then I could leave so I reached around and started tugging. It felt like a baby calf's udder. At least he couldn't see the look of displeasure on my face with me turned the other way.

After what felt like ten hours I finally started feeling him getting firm. It still didn't grow much but I went to move onto my back to proceed with the sex. Before I could move he was done. He came all up my back. Cheers pal. I acknowledged it and asked him to confirm what had just happened and he replied with a laugh and a "yeah sorry" before getting some tissue and wiping me down.

We dressed and left immediately after, passing through the hotel lobby we'd seen 100 times the night before which was now full to capacity with Chinese tourists. What a start to their holiday, seeing us roll out of the lift and onto the bright street outside. He tried to have a full goodbye snog but I pecked him quickly and politely before lumbering off in the opposite direction. Thank god it was still early enough to only have a few people around, less people to see me doing this walk of shame. Had it been a more successful night I'd have called it the stride of pride but we weren't anywhere near that.

I got home, got into bed, plugged my phone into charge (which had died again) and then saw I had a text from my friend telling me he had a girlfriend. She really needs to teach him to be good in bed. Maybe she tried and he's a lost cause. Maybe she doesn't like sex. Maybe he should have just gone home to her and jizzed up her back instead.

And that concluded The Week of Shit Men. One bad date, one horrendously bad date, and one stay in a hotel room with a fat man and his tiny penis. My clitoris felt like it had been treated like a dog toy and I continued to heave at the thought of sucking him off for days. God give me strength.

Another One Plays the Long Game

Mr RE Man sent me a message on Plenty of Fish on the 19th August. We got on really well from the outset, and even though he seemed to be a bit of a character and I couldn't work him out my natural instinct for loving a challenge kicked in and I set to figuring him out straight away. His profile said he was 28, lived in the same town as me, and he told me he worked in a school out of town as an RE teacher. He also said he had a chihuahua, was covered in tattoos, and looked slightly different in all of his pictures.

My level of intrigue meant I pursued it. The filth came out fairly quickly but we had a laugh over text and I felt comfortable being my usual weird self as he seemed to appreciate it. He told me he was half-Italian and took to calling me Bella all the time, and didn't say much about his home life apart from that he lived with one other person, his mum was in a different town with the step-dad he didn't get on with, and his real dad had died when he was one.

There was something strange about him and I couldn't put my finger on what it was. Every time I suggested meeting he came back with 'soon' and never seemed to sleep. His time stamp in the morning was always around 4am yet he replied when I text him at 7am, never mentioned his housemate, and only ever spoke about one friend he had who apparently lived in London. There was one time when he sent me a picture of this friend and a Z list celebrity who they apparently knew and had ended up at the house of after one night out. For someone who was a secondary school teacher he also spent an awful lot of time during the day on his phone, never mentioned lesson planning, but did talk a lot about students and goings on in his classroom so I couldn't decide which way to think.

I seriously considered him to be a catfish until he sent me a Snapchat at my request. Obviously I'd asked for it to clarify he was real but I didn't tell him that. Once his existence was confirmed me and my friends decided he was just massively insecure. He'd told me that back in the day he used to be nicknamed The Heel which apparently means 'the guy who gets all the girls'. But he then told me he hadn't had sex in over six months and hadn't yet met anyone from a dating site so it seemed as though The Heel's luck had ran out. He did make a big point about how much he loved going down on a girl, calling it one of his favourite things ever, and spoke often about how good he was in bed saying his foreplay and technique would definitely make me come. Yeah pal, because it's that easy and I'll fake it if not to make you feel better (no, no, never ever ever).

About a month in, I asked his age again. This time he came back with '26'. How's a man going to lose two years in the space of four weeks? I didn't even question it for some reason or another, just assumed he'd made a mistake somewhere so I now had no clue how old he was.

He hinted at sending me a picture of his penis. I decided to let him make him own mind up on whether he thought it appropriate and he went for it. The picture he sent was also strange. It was blurry; I couldn't work out how he was positioned, and in the middle of his pale body stood a smooth purple penis that looked like Postman Pat's nose. I wasn't waiting forever for this, this was the worst dick pic I'd ever received. It only got worse a few weeks later when he sent another one showing that it wasn't as massive as he thought it was, with wirey untamed pubes lurking around the bottom and the grout on the side of his grubby bathtub clearly on show. This guy was fucking clueless.

When we hit five weeks I started getting pushy. I'd been dating other people and had slept with Mr Kid in the time we were talking and my interest was starting to wilt. Yes we got on well, but I still wasn't sure if I was physically attracted to him as I couldn't decide what he actually looked like in real life from his pictures and I didn't want to play the long game again as it always leads to disappointment. I started thinking there might have been a serious reason he wasn't arranging a meet but I still wanted to meet him just to make sure. I put my foot down and he eventually caved. A date was arranged for the following week, although I could tell it was begrudgingly on his part. He'd already swerved a meet the weekend before due to an apparent root canal, and he said he had a cold the week following to get out of meeting me again.

The day before the date he was acting really off. I knew the date wasn't going to happen and I waited to see what his excuse was. At 5am on the day we were due to meet he sent me a text that read "Morning Sam. I don't want to be a let down and I'm really sorry to do this but I've just had a call from my mum's boyfriend to say she's been in a car crash. He's in China so I have to go and see her, give me any day next week or weekend and I'll be there I promise". I didn't even know what to do with this. He'd told me his mum is a retired teacher so I found it quite unbelievable that she'd been ragging her car around in the early hours but you can't argue with that kind of excuse so I simply replied with "I hope she's ok". He came back later on and told me she was in a terrible state. Broken bones, head to toe bruising, the works, and I was still sceptical which almost made me feel like a terrible human being.

He didn't mention meeting again so a week later I asked him what he was doing that weekend. He said something about 'wanting my pussy' (gross) and I replied with "speaking of that, what are you doing this weekend?" - clearly a meet suggestion to any normal person. He said something about having me 'soon', told me he was watching the baseball on one of the days, and didn't offer to see me another day or ask what I was doing. Great.

After this, I'd well and truly had enough. We were approaching seven weeks by this point and it was getting ridiculous. I still wasn't sure about him and there were things that didn't add up so I decided to ignore him. He text me on the Friday, I ignored it. He then sent me Snapchat videos of him screaming over the baseball which again I ignored. The next night I went out, got real drunk, and when he text asking why he was getting the vibe I didn't want to talk to him anymore I told him I didn't because I was sick of his 'soon' and didn't believe he was ever going to meet me.

A few texts were exchanged and I drunk dialled him about 100 times. I told him I was coming back to his and he suddenly decided he'd stayed over at his friends out of town despite not mentioning that sooner. It was during one of my drunk dials that he asked when he was seeing me and I said Tuesday. However, the next day Tuesday was changed to Wednesday as apparently he had a meeting at school. Tuesday came around and he was still texting all day. So much for this meeting he had.

That night, the night before we were due to meet, he called me. He started talking about going home together and was really pushing the point across. He mentioned coming back to mine despite me living at home and him having his own place down the road, and started asking about the dress code before telling me he was wearing zebra print trousers. He'd also recently bleached his hair yet had dark stubble so his head looked like it had been fucking dip dyed. The chances of me fancying were going downhill rapidly. This is why the long game is never a good idea. He assumed I was going to shag him just because we'd been talking for ages and had got on well over text, whereas I just wanted to see if I actually liked him in person and wasn't thrilled about the idea of him putting his Postman Pat's nose inside me. Still, it looked like I was actually going to meet him which was one turn up for the books.

The Hazy Date with Mr RE Man

On the morning of the date with Mr RE Man he text me saying he'd got croissants in for breakfast the next day. It wasn't until this moment that I felt nervous. He wasn't going to let me go home that night, he had it all figured out.

Through the day we jokingly kept asking each other how nervous the other was out of ten and I kept saying zero until finally admitting his breakfast comment had affected me. It was at this point he admitted he hadn't really got the food in, but still didn't give any of the "You don't have to come home with me if you don't want to". I was clearly going to be having sex, whether I fancied him or not. It's a good job I can shag people I'm not attracted to because if I didn't like him I'd be fucked.

Whilst I was getting ready he told me he'd ended up on the other side of town and asked if we could meet slightly later. I assumed he was at a friend's house as he said he'd had a couple of warm up drinks and found it a bit strange he was predrinking for a date. Still, we already know he clearly needed some Dutch courage and that he's weird so it didn't seem too unbelievable.

He'd planned out the whole night before we even got there. Told me he'd be inside with a gin and tonic waiting for me, told me he was going to kiss me after one drink, and told me all the positions we'd be doing later on in explicit detail. The pressure was on and I wasn't comfortable with how organised he was about the whole thing, but when I arrived and found him lurking outside without a gin and tonic I thought maybe the evening would pan out differently to how he was expecting.

During one of our previous conversations he'd told me he was 5'10", and his POF profile had said 5'11" so that was one inch lost. In real life he was no bigger than 5'6". Another lie. His conversation wasn't nearly as good as it had been over text and he possessed my least favourite man quality. Had no idea what he was doing in his own skin. His body language was odd and awkward, whether he was nervous I don't know but I didn't fancy him at all.

Hedging his bets, he got me straight onto the doubles when we got there which normally I wouldn't do. As we sat with our drinks he probably would have said nothing had I not been desperately squeezing chat out by initiating people watching and talking about other shit just to fill the gaps. The fact it took him seven weeks to meet me was brought up and he replied with "We wouldn't have got on this well if I met you a week after messaging you though". This well?! Yeah pal, I'm having a great time, can hardly get a word in edgeways.

Despite his awkward silence he still managed to say "You are so hot by the way" whilst looking at me like he'd won the lottery and putting his hands all over me within half an hour of being there. I knew I didn't fancy him but I almost felt obliged to let him because of how long we'd been talking and his forwardness, plus the gin was getting all up in my head so I refrained from telling him to fuck off. Had I been sober however, I wouldn't have been comfortable with his handsy action.

It was at some point around a drink and a half that I asked how old he was again. This time he came back with 25. So confused by all that is going on. I couldn't even guess an age by the way he looked either. He was one of those people that could easily be either really young or really old or somewhere in between. His fucking bleached hair and zebra print jeans didn't give much away.

Shortly after, and no doubt to distract me, he lunged at me. I kissed him back because I was drunk and because fuck it and it wasn't long before his conversation started happening.

His conversation however mainly went along the lines of asking me if I was going back with him. Over and over and over again. Two hours later I was properly drunk and I caved. Fine, I was going back with him. Even though it was a school night and I was already going to be hungover at work, now I was going to have to add crippling tiredness and sex ache onto that as well.

We left and he came out with "You're going to call me a presumptuous bastard now" as I already had been all day. He confessed he'd got a hotel room and that was where he'd been before meeting me. I accused him of having a secret wife and he claimed it was because his walls were paper thin and he didn't want his housemate to hear everything. So off we went, to a sterile budget hotel on the other side of town.

Sex was obviously going to happen so I rolled with it. I took my clothes off while he was in the bathroom and waited for all the foreplay he'd promised due to his love of cunnilingus. He went down on me for about 30 seconds before shoving it in and coming within five minutes, screaming "OH SAM" at the top of his lungs. At one point I think he also said "I love being inside you" just like Mr Out of Proportion had so that was a blast from the past. Other utterances included "OH BABY" and some that I just blocked out.

    I didn't look at his penis closely enough to see if it looked like Postman Pat's nose but I could tell it definitely wasn't as big as he thought it was. I put it in my mouth briefly and although it was bigger than Mr Tiny Penis' finger dick, it was still underwhelming. Another big turn off was the sight of his fat belly and the solid defining line beneath. What is with me attracting men with verandas? I do not want a shelter hanging over the toy shop. He kept telling me I have amazing tits and an amazing body; compliments which I couldn't reciprocate because nothing about him or his technique was at all impressive.

    Regardless of this, we ended up having sex about five times. I can only assume this is because he lasted minutes every time and no urge of mine was satisfied. He even started shoving it in dry towards the end. So much for all this foreplay I was getting. He may have lost his erection once or twice as well.

I got up and had a cigarette out the window and when I returned he said "I love that my girl smokes". Your what now? I corrected him and he said "Well you will be my girl in a week!" "No I will not" I replied and he came back with "Oh you want it sooner do you?!" "Absolutely not!" I said. Fucking hell mate, hold your horses.

In the morning, after about three hours of sleep, I got up and called a taxi immediately. I vaguely remember him not feeling like a sleeping person for most of the night apart from the ten minutes he was snoring before waking me up for round six so I'm not even sure if he slept. He may well have just been spooning me naked all night whilst picturing our life together. Whilst I was getting dressed he told me I had to send him a serious text when I was home because I was completely unable to be serious or be soppy the night before, to which I replied "Fuck off, stop trying to change me" and we laughed.

He text me within five minutes of me being in the taxi and we continued to text through the day. He'd told me he was upset he couldn't make me come and I told him I wasn't going to fake it so he claimed it would be his new mission. I swear these men think I'm just an anomaly who doesn't come from being prodded for a few minutes, when in reality they've probably been with a lot of girls who have faked it, leading them to believe they're amazing. Fuck that. These men need educating, not their egos stroked. If I'm not getting off then I'm not going to let you walk around like Billy Big Bollocks thinking you're God's gift to women.

We continued to text over the next few days but while my hangover subsided and my straight thoughts kicked in I started thinking this might not be a good idea after all.

The Aftermath and a Series of Unanswered Questions

When the weekend came round, Mr RE Man hadn't mentioned meeting again. After him calling me 'his girl' and getting meet one out of the way I suppose I expected him to move a bit quicker, but he wasn't and my interest in this situation was starting to die.

On the Saturday, two weeks after his mother's apparently horrific car crash, he told me he was out for lunch with her. Now I've never been in a car crash or broken any bones but I would have thought someone in that kind of state wouldn't be able to get up and swan off for lunch two weeks later. This was one step too far on the dodgy stakes so I started doing what I do best… internet lurking to try and find out who the hell this guy was.

I started by looking up his full Italian name. According to Google no one in the whole world of this name exists, and Google knows everyone and everything so that was that. I then remembered how another name variation was used on a picture of prescribed pills on his Instagram (insomnia apparently). I then looked that name up. I found his Facebook which was still open and which said he'd gone to a college miles away, and not long after that I found a Linked.in profile of a lecturer there of the same name. Weird. That was nowhere near where we live, or where he apparently works.

Then I found his Twitter which was private but said he was in the location where he worked and had a link to a banking website. That's odd for a teacher who used to work in banking, why would he still have that link? The picture on his profile was a recent baseball one too so it couldn't be said he hadn't used it for ages.

I noticed we had a mutual friend on Facebook and debated sending him a message to ask what he knew but wasn't sure how weird that would be considering I hadn't spoken to said mutual friends in years. I kept that as an idea for if we got really stuck.

All of this had fully turned me against him. On the Monday he asked if I wanted to go to a gig which was a month away, like that would be the next time I saw him. When I told him I was already at another gig that night he replied with "Well I didn't really want to go anyway", then later on started telling me about how I should talk to him about my feelings. Fuck off mate, I've met you once I'm not telling you anything about my feelings over this weird text relationship that you're trying to create. That was the nail in the coffin, I needed to get rid.

It was after this that I decided to bite the bullet and message the mutual friend. His advice? "If it were me, I'd steer clear". Worrying.

To wind me up even more, after I stopped replying he sent me another commentary stream of texts about the baseball, two Snapchat videos of the same, and three crying faces the next day. The day after that I received the last text from him. "Haha ok if u don't reply this time I'll leave u to it cos I know you've had a busy wk but u clearly don't wanna spk to me anymore… I'd just rather know why n move on" apologies for the poor spelling but apparently that's the kind of people teaching the children of our generation these days. I debated texting back, decided to leave it until the morning, then thought 'nah' and never spoke to him again. One good thing of him can be said here, and that's that he stuck to his word and did piss off forever.

I never found out who he actually was, what he did, how old he was, or any of the other unanswered questions but a few weeks after it was all over I had another look on his Twitter and he'd opened it to public view. Naturally I scrolled back to the day we met. I found a couple of tweets from the night we were out together. They went as follows… "#HEEL that's all you need to know", funny as he'd protested against him being 'The Heel' these days, yet there he was fucking hashtagging it while I was probably in the toilet, "WEDNESDAY NIGHT IN PITCHER IS A REAL EVENT" yep, that's where we were, and "PITCHER. NOT BASEBALL. WHAT ARE THE ODDS? Fugged". The next day he'd tweeted the picture he'd sent me in the morning with "Far too many Red Stripes last night (it was three pints) best night out in months", then "Keep pulling rabbits" later on, whatever the fuck that means.

The crescendo came on the evening of the day after. He'd uploaded a screen shot of a conversation which went as follows:

Mr RE Man: "I need some advice from The Badger (yeah he called his mate that). Would you shag a Spanish 6 just to get you into parties for free? I mean she's okish but she's like minted and seems to party for a living."

The Badger: Course I fucking would! Heel it! Dilemma is though, can you hack at other birds if you're with her?

Mr RE Man: "That's exactly it mate."

HACK AT?! FUCKING HACK AT?!?! Sorry mate but you're not doing any kind of fucking hacking with that tiny Postman Pat nose purple fucking penis. Yeah alright, you had a few goes but you didn't even make a dent. The only damage you caused that night was to MY FUCKING DIGNITY. Yeah I'm furious. What even is this person?! I'd started to feel a bit bad about the way I pied him off but now this Gunther wannabe with his fucking bleached hair, terrible dress sense, overhanging gut and distinct lack of real life personality can get fucked.

Ok so after that outburst I later realised that was a screenshot from November 2012 (whut?). But I still stand by everything I said as his on-the-night tweets were a joke. He was not that pissed after three pints. Dickhead.

A Touch of Déjà vu

Another October night out ended up exactly how a night out a few weeks ago planned out. Yep, in a hotel room. However, this time it was marginally better than the last experience.

I picked up a 21 year old half Indian boy in the same stomping ground as the last Saturday night's (attempted) shag. He was good looking, had good chat, and danced like he took his clothes off for money. He'd told me he'd be the best I'd ever had shortly before arrangements for leaving together were made. Originally, Mr Half Indian Kid had told me he worked in IT but he felt the need to tell me he lied and he actually worked in a gym just before we walked out the door like it was that much of a big deal. I didn't care where he worked, as long as he put in a better performance than the past couple of conquests and didn't expect me to pay for the hotel as I was running on empty as far as my bank account was concerned.

We had a laugh and it was when we were walking towards McDonald's for a pre-shag snack that I said "So you're going to be the best I've ever had are you?" "Probably not" he replied. You've got to respect that level of honesty. We sat eating burgers with his friend and his girlfriend (his treat) before making our way over to the hotel for the night. Bad luck, they were out of rooms. We got in a taxi and went to another hotel. They were fully booked too, and told us their other branch was also out of bounds for the night. Shit.

There was a hotel across the road but it was swanky as fuck and I wasn't sure if they'd accept two horny, drunken louts but we gave it a go anyway. £100 later and after a conversation about whether or not I wanted him to pay £11 for the breakfast (obviously wanted, but I declined), we were in.

I'll be honest, I don't remember a great deal about the act but what I do remember is he did zero foreplay. That probably worked in his favour as it made him feel bigger. He seemed to be scared of touching my genitals or tits with his hands or mouth, but he did last fucking ages. I remember him waking me up at one point but I'm not sure if this was halfway through or in between rounds one and two. All kinds of positions were cracked out and he managed to sustain an erection throughout it all. I also remember him saying "I never want it to end" just before he finally came. There was a point where he said something along the lines of "We'll definitely be doing this again" but he used long words and I didn't quite understand what he meant so he had to explain his grammatical choices whilst banging me which would have been horrendously awkward should we both have been sober.

In the morning we had another round. He pulled me on top of him and put it in without foreplay again. But still, he was doing well compared to anyone else I'd been in contact with recently so we were all good. He came a bit quicker that time and we had some forced conversation before I decided it was time to go home and stumbled around the room shamelessly naked trying to find my underwear.

He got up and gave me a hug goodbye which was strange and I left. Another Sunday doing the walk of shame. I didn't hear from him again so his sentence explanation was completely null and void. Still, the sex was good enough to satisfy me for at least a day so something was achieved out of all this.

If in Doubt, Get 'em Out for the Delusional Men

Once again I'd found myself with no man options. Once again, I panicked. I could probably write a whole chapter about how ten solid months of online dating has had a very unhealthy impact on my emotional wellbeing and about how, before this year, I never used to feel hugely disappointed when I woke up to no texts or messages from men but I won't. It's all true, but I'm putting it down to the fact I've become massively focused on this book being amazing and no messages means no characters which means no chapters. And that of course equals no content and no book. I've become the person I was in January, all business-only. Except now I feel slightly more educated on the men of my generation, have fewer inhibitions when it comes to dirty talk and naked pictures between myself and strangers, and am slightly more dead inside.

      This leads me nicely onto telling you what I did next. Before I met Mr RE Man I'd taken a fairly tasteful topless picture of myself. My hands were holding my tits so there was no nipple on show (and to hold them up so they weren't touching my knees), I had the bottom of my face visible sporting a pout, and had added a nice filter to it, naturally. I was trying to sum up the courage and the excuse to put it on a Tinder moment, to my 200 matches, in the hope of getting some interest. The excuse came in the form of 'No Bra Day'. I took the plunge, and unsurprisingly it got more likes than any picture of my face ever had. The messages rolled in, which they hadn't before (am I butters though?) and the talkers were quickly transferred to text and Snapchat.

However, talkers were all they were. In fact I'm not even going to bother giving them names for their time wasting. No interest in meeting, not even for sex, just wanted dirty talk and pictures. One sent me a picture of his penis which looked like a fucking meatloaf and another one, despite being unbelievably good looking, sent me the worst dick pic I've ever seen. It was from up top, was in the slightest semi-state, was absolutely tiny, massively veered off to the left, and looked like it had a layer of skin peeled off it. I wish I could show you all a picture of it as everyone I did show genuinely heaved. After I opened that in the morning I was in a foul mood all day, stopped replying to his texts, and took a two week man break because I was fucking furious at how anyone can think that's sexy. Delusional fucking men. I'd say that's the equivalent of me standing naked in front of a mirror, gunt out, nipples pointing down and sending that around. Do me a fucking favour.

There seems to be a lot of these digital-only men about. They'll be all over it for a few days, get as much as they can, then disappear (if I haven't already disappeared on them) and I assume move onto the next one. I'm not a man so I don't know their reasons for this behaviour but I will say these people need a fucking hobby. If you're lurking on Tinder just to get pictures of girls' tits and for them to say things for you to wank off to with no intention of meeting them then you need to take a look at your life and reassess. Get outside. Go for a walk. Or stay in and watch porn. Either way, piss off and stop wasting my energies.

Part of me thinks that these men do it because they get to pretend to be something they're not, something better than they are. Their dirty talk always goes along the lines of "I'd do this and you'd fucking love it." "You'll be dripping wet." "And then you come." First off, don't tell me how I'm going to be feeling, you don't know me. Secondly, if all men think we women come that easily then we've got a real big problem on our hands.

I don't know whether this is just what happens in their heads, but I fear this may be what they say due to previous women they've slept with faking it. I've spoken to a lot of females about the faking it thing, trawled women's magazines in search of faking it debates, and it seems like a large percentage do it. This needs to stop. Why should we be pretending just so we don't bruise the man on top of us' ego? We deserve to come just as much as they do, we owe it to ourselves to orgasm after letting a man all up in our personal space, so rather than fake it can't we just teach men that *it's not that fucking easy.* Let's re-educate them together. Let's make sex as good for us as it is for them. Let's stop thinking about *their* feelings. Are they really that bothered about us once they're pounding away? In my experience, no not really. I've never met a man who can't come because he's so upset about the woman not coming first. Sure, they've said they love making a woman come over and over again in the pre-meet stage but it's not mentioned again until after they're done and suddenly they're upset it didn't happen. I have never faked it, I never will, and when a man does express his disappointment I make it very clear that I'm not going to start faking it just for them.

When (if) the day comes that I meet the right person, I'd hope he's not full of empty sex promises and does all he can to make me come. Not so he can mentally high five himself for being 'the man who cracked it' or for winning the challenge, but because he likes and respects me enough to do everything possible to make sure I'm up there reaching climax with him. Or before him, or after him, or any fucking time. And in exchange, on the days my sensitivity has fallen into a coma or I'm not feeling it, I'll make sure he knows I enjoyed it all the same, because he'll know that it's about the journey and not the destination, and because he'll know either from me or a previous woman who's taught him well that we do still have a nice time rolling around naked with a human being we fancy and that we don't need the earth to move to prove it.

Real life sex isn't how we thought it would be when we were growing up, or how it looks in the films. If two people have ever come at the same time during their first time together and after five minutes I want to fucking meet them. And anyway, if sex really was like that it wouldn't be anywhere near as awkwardly fun as it is for us on planet earth.

The Date That Made Me Question My Life

The start of November saw another returner that hadn't previously been mentioned. When we first exchanged words months prior to now, Mr Pretend Gentleman had pissed me off by catching me on a bad day and making a joke about me being a lingerie model. When he messaged again, he acknowledged his shanter (shit banter) and it became clear that's just how he rolled. I started to find him fairly amusing, despite him being incredibly erratic, and we went on to have long phone calls in the evening as well as texting all day long.

A date was set quickly. It was arranged for him to come to me and for us to go for dinner and drinks. However, in the days leading up to our meet he was reminded of a wedding he was meant to go to instead. Rather than apologise and reschedule me, he had the great idea of trying to make me go to the wedding with him. We hadn't met at this point and although everyone likes the idea of a spontaneous date, in real life that would just be fucking weird. I couldn't cope with the thought of his friends asking how long we'd been together or where we met, and didn't love the idea of being in pictures and being forever referred to as 'that bird off Tinder he'd taken with him'. I refused to go, and he then came up with another plan.

He lived on his own in a town half an hour away and decided that we'd have a much better time there. He suggested coming to pick me up, riding the train back with me if I didn't want to stay, calling me a taxi, ordering a horse and cart to pick me up from my house, getting a coach to mine then walking back. Ok I got carried away there, but the amount of different transport options he offered was bizarre. All to get me to go to his. I told him I knew he was trying to bamboozle me into staying over and that I knew what would happen if we were both drunk but he insisted on me staying in the spare room, claiming he'd be the perfect gentleman and would show me an amazing time.

I didn't really care where we went. I'm not impressed by venues and places, and am a firm believer in the success of the night all being measured against the company rather than the location. Regardless of this, I caved to his insistence. After a day of going on and not letting up against my protests I opted for an easier life and agreed to go to his place, saying I'd be staying in his spare room. He did have a really awesome dog to be fair, so the temptation of meeting him swayed me.

I already had plans for the day after, and had hair and eyebrow appointments for the afternoon on the day so I knew we were set to a time limit which put me at ease. Mr Pretend Gentleman came to pick me and my suitcase up from the train station with a bunch of flowers in tow, and on the drive back to his he somehow got onto the subject of drugs. He asked if I dabbled, to which I replied "occasionally" and he made the suggestion of getting a gram of coke. I made it very clear that I was not keen due to being in a town that I didn't know with a man I'd only just met and I thought he'd laid that idea to rest.

We went straight to his before going out for the evening. Sitting and chatting over a drink on his sofa was odd, made no easier by the fact he was sat up straight directly opposite me and staring at me in a bewildered way. He was knocking back the booze as we chatted and he told me the plan for the evening. Our first stop was dinner at a Slovakian restaurant, followed by a Caribbean themed bar, and the last destination was to be an Alice in Wonderland tea party themed cocktail place. I still didn't really give a shit about where we were going, but he had ignored all previous protests about my lack of interest in venue and tried to impress me regardless.

He showed me up to his spare room so I could get ready for the evening ahead. The dog came and sat in with me, and it was at this moment I stopped and realised what I was doing. I had travelled to another town to go out with a man I'd met an hour ago, and was currently getting ready in his spare room with his fucking dog while he was upstairs doing the same. What the fuck is this. When we regrouped it soon became clear that he was going to try every possible tactic and every possible personality to see which one worked best.

After the awkward one I was greeted with, the alcohol kicked in during our break and he'd morphed into an arrogant arsehole. Mr Pretend Gentleman kept going on about how incredibly good looking he was (he wasn't) and generally behaved like one of the pretentious wankers I usually try to avoid. I'm not usually in the house of said pretentious wankers so avoiding them is never too difficult. This time, however, I was trapped.

The pretentious wanker act lasted all the way to the restaurant and all through dinner. He grabbed me and kissed me on the way there so I knew there was only ever going to be one outcome from this date, with his agreement of me staying in the spare room being suspected bullshit as I'd thought.

During dinner I tried to loosen up and get into the swing of it but my bad mood meant that I wasn't being affected by the alcohol at all. We started talking about holidays and I told him about my time in Sicily when an Italian family fed me up all week. He interrupted with "I can tell" before getting in a strop because I wouldn't let him take a picture of me over the table after obviously just calling me fat.

It was also during dinner that he claimed he thought I was joking when I said I didn't want any cocaine, and that he'd already put an order in with someone who was on their way. Fucking marvellous. I got angry and asked how he could have possibly read my "absolutely not" as a joke, and he started claiming he'd get into trouble if he ignored his dealer and didn't go and pick up. I ate my dinner with steam pouring out of my ears before we moved onto the Caribbean bar which was not as good as he'd claimed. He also left me alone in there for 15 minutes while he went to collect the drugs I didn't want. So far, so shit.

When he got back he suggested going home as he couldn't afford the table at the Alice in

Wonderland place now he'd paid for the other stuff. I'd given up on trying to have a good time so agreed, and got into my pyjamas as soon as I got back. The coke, like the alcohol, wasn't affecting me at all. He, on the other hand, was off his fucking tits.

The drugs made him go from arrogant wanker to insecure fuck in 0.5 seconds. Whilst sat there rolling his tongue around his disgustingly dry mouth, making the noises to match, he tried to insinuate a deep and meaningful conversation. He started telling me all about the breakdown of his parent's marriage, the difficult relationship he'd shared with his father, and the awful financial situations that had arisen which lead to them being unable to restore the swimming pool in their garden. When it came to my turn to share a sad and harrowing story from my life, I swiftly told him to piss off.

We had put The X Factor on and, when the coke had dried up, he made the suggestion to go and watch it in his room. Oh I wonder why. This mug definitely thought I was born yesterday. But of course I went because I was in his house and didn't want to argue with him. So much for me staying in the spare room. I wasn't feeling particularly horny after all of the evening's events but he put his head under the cover to 'go and explore' and once he'd started sucking my nipples I was as wet as an otters pocket. He'd found my weak spot. He then worked his way down before proving himself to be something of an oral champion. For all his other failings (everything about him) his cunnilingus skills were up there. I came within minutes which is incredibly impressive considering I hated the sight of him.

He got on top and popped himself in, and I was suddenly back to disliking him again. His penis was like a fucking pencil, long and thin. It wasn't until he properly started pounding that I felt something, but that could have just been the force of impact. He stayed on top of me and claimed he was 'holding off on coming'. Just what I needed, cheers pal. He was a fairly large man in build and there was no way I could have moved from beneath him due to him putting all of his weight on top of me. That didn't stop him from going back to arrogant wanker briefly afterwards by claiming I just lied there and took it. Well I did, but I didn't have much sodding choice in the matter.

As we went to sleep, he tried to spoon me and mumbled "why are you so brilliant?" before I wriggled out of his clutches. He got the hump and rolled over, sleeping with his back to me which was probably the second best part of the evening after the motting out.

The morning after, I felt absolutely fine. He was hanging out of his arsehole. Despite his hangover, he still went down on me again which I found quite surprising considering he'd blown his load bareback inside me a few hours previously. I came again, and again he shuffled his pencil into my case for a quick one. I got up, showered, and faffed about a bit before waking him up again and forcing him to feed me because I was starving. Going back to a reasonably decent human being, he got up and went to the shop before cooking me a bacon sandwich as I chilled with his dog on the sofa.

When the time came to leave, he asked if I'd had a nice time and if I wanted to see him again. I agreed reluctantly before getting my train.

Following our meeting, he started taking hours to reply to my texts and was being really off with me. This guy clearly thought I'd be a needy girl who falls in love after having sex with someone, and that I'd chase the shit out of him. Wrong girl, pal. After a day of shit texts I stopped replying completely. He realised his wrong doings and came back with his tail between his legs, asking why I'd gone quiet. As if you needed to ask. I didn't reply to the other few messages he sent either which no doubt dented his ego. It was a shame such good oral skills went to waste on such an appalling human being.

Changing My Dating Technique

I first started talking to Mr Normal in August but due to cancellations on both of our parts we didn't meet until the week after I saw Mr Pretend Gentleman in November. He had fairly good chat, didn't particularly excite me, but didn't throw up any major red flags either. He was funny, didn't sway too much into the filth-zone, and generally just seemed normal.

After the dates I'd had recently, I decided I was fed up with spending the day getting nervous and rushing after work whilst getting ready, only to end up resenting the men I'd met for wasting my time and energies for nothing. Due to this, when the day finally came to meet Mr Normal I didn't wash my hair, didn't make as much effort with my makeup, and put on a dress that didn't show my tits or my shape at all. Quite frankly, I couldn't be fucking bothered. Typically this was the one date, in hindsight, that I wish I had made myself look hot as shit for.

We met in a quiet bar in town and got through half the cocktail list, all paid for by him without any protests. The chat flowed and we had a laugh but I could feel that I wasn't quite myself. This guy was making me nervous and I couldn't even look him in the eye properly. His size and build was perfect, he was much better looking in real life than I expected, and he was normal in the best way possible.

He worked in a similar industry to me so we had a lot to talk about in that respect, and we exchanged funny stories about our friends and nights out. I really liked him, and I rarely like anyone so I started panicking about a pie before I'd even left him. Of course, I didn't say this to him or address the fact I looked like shit.

When the time came to say goodbye, he gave me a hug and we parted ways. There was no talk of seeing each other again and no awkward lurking. As I sat waiting for my bus home I got a sinking feeling and knew that, despite having a good time, I wouldn't see him again. And of course, I was right. I didn't hear from him the next day so I sent him the message the day after. He replied a few times, but made no conversation whatsoever. In the time between now and the date I had also stalked all of his social media and discovered he'd only been single for a few months. His ex was incredible, she looked like Mila fucking Kunis. I can't compare to that, and his short time of being single probably meant he wasn't sure how to properly throw a pie so I'll let him off for trying to phase me out.

After eleven months of dating I finally meet someone seemingly normal who I'm ridiculously attracted to and he's not interested. Of course he bloody isn't.

The Final Stretch

As December approached, I was holding out hope for luck to take hold and to send me my Prince Charming to ride off into the sunset with at the end of the book. I had a few options but none were giving off the Possibility Vibe apart from one who I was interested in, despite him being a seemingly slow mover. After three weeks of talking I went quiet on him, knowing which way it would push him and I was right. He text me again and asked if I wanted to go for a drink the following week.

On the day of meeting, he didn't text me with plans until 4pm. Men seem to do this a lot, surely I'm not the only person who thinks this takes the piss a bit and likes to know what they're doing a bit earlier than that. I didn't want to double tap to arrange and he seemed to have no problem with the late arrangements when he eventually did get in touch, giving him his name of Mr Laidback.

When we met I quickly noticed that he didn't tick any of the assets on my top three list. His hair was barely there and potentially thinning, his lips weren't particularly full, and I couldn't really make his arms out but he didn't look the type to have big manly guns. Regardless of this, I was still fairly attracted to him as he seemed genuinely nice and cool. In the first bar he did go to the toilet a lot within a short space of time which I found slightly odd, but I later discovered he shared my bad habit of being a smoker and he was actually just sneaking off for that and found it more appropriate to pretend he had a weak bladder than admit where he was going.

Moving onto the second bar I already felt slightly tipsy which was handy because when we got to our destination it was full of people I knew from work. Awkward. It soon emerged that someone I knew from work had been good friends with Mr Laidback at university. What a small world. We then ended up joining them where he sat and caught up with his old friend as the rest of the table gawped at him trying to work him out.

We went for a food pit stop and ended up eating a Subway at a bus stop like a really classy pair. His was full of all the terrible menu options as he had sat back and allowed me to ruin his food as I customised it in the worst way, finding it hilarious. We also found it hilarious to follow a pair of kids to the worst bar in town after hearing the one who looked like Barney Rubble proclaim he'd definitely pull in there. We ended up in the middle of a dancefloor surrounded by youths six years our junior and it was there that we had our first kiss. His technique could have used some work. Overall, it was a bit too quick for my liking. Not in terms of time, but in terms of pace and rhythm. I think I tried to slow it down at some point but he didn't really follow my lead.

By the time we got to our last stop we were both absolutely hammered. We ended up making friends with a random group of people who shouted "TINDERRR" at us when we kissed after telling them where we met, and I was introduced to his sister's boyfriend. When we left, we were snogging against a railing outside before he asked me to go back to his. He lived at home with his parents still so I wasn't sure how much I wanted to meet them in the morning but I also hadn't shaved any part of my body in preparation for potential sex. There was something in me whilst getting ready that just said I didn't want to do it if it arose. Maybe because of the poor quality of people I'd slept with recently, maybe because Christmas was approaching and I felt really soft around the edges. I'm not really sure, but I knew it was a no.

We parted ways and continued to talk through the week. Despite having a good, eventful date however, the chat didn't even slightly ramp up. There was no flirt, no filth, and just nothing of interest really. He would text me every day asking how my day had been but when you work 8.30am to 5pm in a relatively boring job where one day doesn't particularly differ from the next, there's only so many times you can put up with that question.

  The next week we went out again. Unfortunately I was on my period so I already knew we wouldn't be going home together this time either so my attendance was slightly begrudging. The conversation was slow, just as it had been in the texts, and he soon invited all of his friends to join us. I seemed to find it easier to speak to his friends than I did with him, and yet he still sat with his hand on my leg in front of them and would kiss me when we were alone. I had a night out for a friend's birthday planned the following evening and soon cashed in the excuse to leave early. He walked me to a taxi and was halfway through a kiss goodbye when he asked if he could grab my arse. I held back from telling him to grow some balls and to just fucking do it, and gave him permission instead.

  The chat after the second date still didn't get any more exciting. Mr Laidback and his lack of anything to say was really starting to grate on me but for some reason I decided I'd at least sleep with him and see if it awoke some life in him. Some kind of higher power was forcing me to be traditional and wait until the third date to have sex. I put my boredom down to not seeing his penis and persevered.

The third date was set for us to meet after my work Christmas meal. I woke up at 6.30am that morning to shave my body in preparation and started my night with a Sambuca to get me going. We met in a bar where all of my work colleagues were. He had a friend in the crowd and although we spent some time together, apparently a lot of his time was spent at the bar necking tequilas. Maybe he was nervous and panic drank, but he was absolutely fucking wasted very quickly. We went to another bar where more people from work were, and he swayed about unable to have any kind of conversation with anyone. Then he fell asleep standing up. Fantastic.

I was fucking fuming. I did not wake up at half 6 to shave my muff for this. I told him to leave and a workmate eventually stepped in and escorted him out. He then text me two hours later asking where I was, telling me he was in another bar. What the hell, man. The next day he text me with some bollocks about feeling shit and I let him sweat all day before replying and mentioning his behaviour which finally gained an apology. I left it a few days again before texting him and pieing him off. I was no longer interested in sticking it out to see the size of his dong, I was bored shitless with his chat, and I realised he wasn't going to be the end of book Prince Charming I was hoping for.

New Year, New Me

As I entered into 2015 I had deleted all online dating profiles, sacked off all men I'd been speaking to, and was officially on my own with the view of staying that way for the first time in over a year. It felt odd but it felt needed. I took a vow of celibacy, claiming I had no intention of meeting anyone any time soon. After the grief that men had put me through last year, I needed time out.

I had met 20 men in 2014. That's a lot of men over the space of 12 months. I needed to regroup my thoughts, address how cock-hungry I'd become, and think about what I really want.

This was all going well. I woke up to no texts, wasted no time on Tinder, and watched all of Grey's Anatomy from the beginning instead of going on dates. I was fine without dating and without attention. I wasn't missing sex, honestly.

That's what I kept telling myself anyway. And that lasted for a grand total of three weeks. Before this man-break was broken I'd had a dream about Mr Fit Animal Man. In the dream, I was in my Nan's house having a sleepover with some friends downstairs when he came in through the patio doors with his dog and went upstairs to the front bedroom. I joined him. You can guess what happened. I'm not sure where my Nan was meant to be while all this was going down but you can't read too much into dreams, can you?

Three weeks into my celibacy and 'no men' vow, I texted Mr Fit Animal Man when I was drunk. He responded and we started talking again. Constantly. There was even an hour long phone call at one point. He told me the reason he couldn't meet me last year was because he was depressed and that he'd told me that at the end of our last conversation. I obviously never got this message, but apparently he was pissed off for a few days about it.

I was due to move out of my mum's house and into a house share, and we made plans for him to come and see me when I'd settled. Was I finally going to meet this man? The one who I'd always been wondering about, and who I'd been so besotted by despite never meeting him?

It was a Wednesday evening. He'd pulled up outside my house and I went and met him. I could barely see him over the roof of his car. I should have known there'd be something wrong with him and the fact he was a borderline dwarf made it all seem clear. Another man lying about his height, excellent. He came in and I attempted to make him a cup of tea without staring at how tiny he was and how he was not as smouldering and serious as I expected. He made friendly small talk with my housemate whilst trying to stand up tall to reach my shoulders.

When we got upstairs, we chatted for about an hour and watched TV. The height wasn't as much of an issue when we were lying on my bed and we still got on well in person. It felt comfortable but I knew then he wasn't The One. Something just didn't quite click.

The sex though. Yes, sex happened. Of course it fucking did. If you've got this far you know there's no way I'd be alone with a man without getting my vag out. He said before he'd destroy me and that he did. He also destroyed my bed which I made him fix before he left. I'd lived in my new place for one week and I was already destroying the furniture by having rough sex on it. His stamina was the one impressive thing about him, I was howling and he had a trick of being able to carry on after he'd came.

Here I was, on a sober school night completely naked and full up to the hinge of a man I met in real life an hour ago. I was a different person to me 12 months ago but if this dating business has given me anything it's a shitload of confidence and a lot less fucks given which is a pretty awesome thing to come away with.

The sex went on for a few hours before I finished off the final round by sucking him off. My room was dimly lit so we could see each other clearly, which is unfortunate because it meant I couldn't hide the massive face malfunction that followed after he came. His heavy load emptied into my mouth and as I tried to breathe, swallow and heave at the same time, all of his deposit came shooting out of my nose. Seriously. I got the angry dragon out on a casual Wednesday. I tried to catch it with my hands cupped under my face and nakedly stumbled to grab a tissue while he asked "is this actually happening right now?"

I saw him out, we had a few messages after, but we never saw each other again which I'm sure isn't entirely surprising.

And that is how this book ends. With no beautiful story of a mad love affair, no romance, no smooth-running date, just another tragic yet hilarious story to add to my collection; my collection which started this whole idea in the first place. I took on the dating game for a year, I'd lost quite significantly, but I've come out as a person I like more at the end of it. So to all the men I've written about, I'd like to say thank you. No matter how much of an arsehole you were, how badly I treated you, or if we never quite got to meet in real life, you all taught me something in one way or another.

Here's to losing the dating game some more, until Mr Right finally sweeps me off my feet. Or until I die alone in Spinster Mansion surrounded by dogs. Cheers.

Printed in Great Britain
by Amazon.co.uk, Ltd.,
Marston Gate.